Dear Small Church Pastor

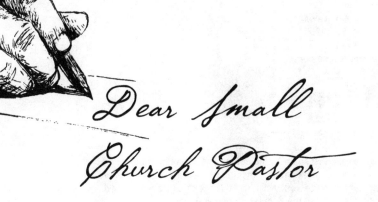

Dear Small Church Pastor

John L. McHaffie

XULON PRESS

Xulon Press
2301 Lucien Way #415
Maitland, FL 32751
407.339.4217
www.xulonpress.com

Paperback ISBN-13: 978-1-66281-921-6
Ebook ISBN-13: 978-1-66281-922-3

Special Thanks

To my wife, Susan McHaffie who has stuck with me in the tough times and the good times. You are my life-partner in this ministry journey, and I would not want to share with anyone but you. Let's keep moving forward, serving, and going wherever the Lord leads us.

Table of Contents

Foreword

John McHaffie is my friend and a man of God. He loves ministering to people. He has a true pastor's heart. I am deeply honored to write this forward.

For as long as I have known him, John has tried to follow the command of Jesus in the great commission to "go into the highways and hedges" and minister to the poor and needy- the hurting and broken. He often finds the forgotten in our communities and presents them with the "Good News" of the gospel through meeting some of their base needs all the while sharing the love of Christ.

John has seen many victories and accomplishments throughout his ministry as a pastor of smaller churches. He also has faced many hurdles and roadblocks in those same churches. His transparency should be a lesson for all of us, in that God is still at work in the place that He has called us to minister.

Every page of this book permeates with the heart of John. If you are a pastor of a smaller church in America, you will be able to identify with the ups and downs- the joys and heartaches that John has faced that has prompted him to write this book. He wants to share his journey with those who may need a spiritual uplift or simply a reminder that we must put our confidence in our God to be the kind of pastor we need to be to reach our communities for Christ.

May the stories, illustrations, and ideas in this book give you encouragement and inspiration through the power of the Holy Spirit.

Blessings,
Jim Calvin, Director of Children's and Discipleship Ministries
Southern Missouri District of the Assemblies of God

Preface

$\mathcal{I}$n this treatise on a seldom explored topic, author John McHaffie has succeeded in capturing very poignantly and very graphically the often unique, specific, and very gut-wrenching, personal struggles of a twenty-first century pastor laboring in virtual anonymity on the often-overlooked rural landscape.

With refreshing and at times, remarkable and unexpected candor, Rev. McHaffie unearths subjects, angst, wounds, and emotions previously kept deeply hidden under the heavy wraps of protective covering. McHaffie here opens healthy, meaningful, and productive dialogue on themes previously dismissed as taboo talk, labeled as "off limits" and "better left unspoken".

In the earthy, folksy, non-threatening literary style of the informal, but deeply personal, vintage snail-mail letter, John struck the right note with the perfect genre for this type of inspirational, therapeutic, and cathartic life-coaching that packs the potential for spiritually nursing the weary, battle-scarred pastoral warrior back to health and wholeness!

This collection of very soul-touching pieces of correspondence is punctuated with genuineness and authenticity that suggests a raw and unvarnished quality! It is rough, honest, and real!

John McHaffie creates a literary work here that is clearly composed with an unapologetic vulnerability and transparency that so perfectly conveys what many rural pastors have so painfully borne inside of them, but never felt like there was a safe forum through which they could divulge it!

In this published work, McHaffie has given a voice of clarity and boldness to the often most misunderstood, underestimated, and maligned under shepherds in our Pentecostal ranks! John comes by this honestly, as his beginnings and formative years were firmly rooted in the rich, fertile soil of America's heartland which helped shape and form his empathetic compassion for and natural identification with the small-town pastor. That pastor who feels he is destined to forever languish in obscurity because he lacks any population center from which to draw from and is often bereft of the technological resources, both of the human and inanimate varieties, that the well-heeled suburban parishes possess in abundance and so casually take for granted!

Rev. McHaffie's well-rounded and balanced perspective from which he approaches this desperately needed project is both organic and diverse. John has served in full-time ministry in urban, suburban, and rural settings in numerous regions of the U.S. spanning multiple states in the Midwest and on the East Coast. So, having experienced the monolithic challenges of these various cultural dynamics firsthand, the sharp contrasts have given John a keen awareness of the plight of choice servants of the harvest master who represent an often marginalized, but oh-so-vital dimension and component to ensuring that the gospel reaches every "Whosoever"!

As a former pastor of John McHaffie's, when he was in early adulthood, I can say I recognized the obvious calling he had on his life to be a loving, nurturing shepherd! As a rural pastor myself at the time, I always knew I could count on and depend on the loyal and enthusiastic support that John would provide for my vision and ministry! He was always a remarkable young man with sterling character, impeccable integrity, and unquestioned passion for the pursuit of greater intimacy with God and Christian service! If this book had been made available to me at that time, it may well have elongated and protracted my tenure in rural ministry! I am certain it would have enabled me to be more patient and more fruitful.

John McHaffie's earnestness and loving concern for the health and vitality of the rural pastor's life and ministry are palpable and resonate here, making the reader feel understood and heard! It's written from the perspective of a Comrade-In-Arms who is offering supportive advocacy to those who now feel reduced to voices lost in the wind of a vast and lonely wilderness.

McHaffie, in this singular composition, validates the rural pastor with the "essential" status that the much more, and deservedly so as well, ballyhooed, highlighted, and spotlighted urban under shepherd has long enjoyed!

I unreservedly, unhesitatingly commend both this book and its author to you! It is a desperately needed and long overdue treatment, most worthy of your time! It will be life-changing for some and even lifesaving for others!! For the discouraged and downtrodden, help is in these pages!! Be encouraged!!

Rev. Steve Schuessler, Lead Pastor
Lighthouse Fellowship
East Brunswick, NJ

Acknowledgments

$\mathcal{E}$ach of us involved in ministry has doubted the words Paul
wrote to his young friend in 1 Timothy 3:1, "**It is a trust-
worthy statement: if any man aspires to the office of overseer, it is a
fine work he desires to do**" (NASB). The pressures, isolation, discouragement and —— can cause us to see ministry not as a *fine
work* but as a frustrating work. This frustration can be compounded
by the seeming success of others in ministry. How does a minister
discover joy, peace and purpose in a vocation which is misunderstood by those he/she serves?

In the pages of this groundbreaking work, you will discover
honest answers to the negative feeling you are experiencing.

John's authenticity and vulnerability can be seen on every page.
His approach will help remove your sense of being alone with
your feelings. Equally important, you will discover a biblical way
of viewing your God given vocation. A way of living out ministry
which includes serving in joy, in peace and on purpose.

In my 30 years of vocational ministry, I have served in rural,
urban, and suburban congregations. I can honestly say that the
principles laid out in the pages of this book apply to you regardless
of your location. The following pages will help you understand why
Paul told Timothy that our office of overseer is a *fine work*.

Dr. Stephen Zemanek
Lead Pastor, Praise Assembly of God
Des Peres, MO

1 Thessalonians 3:6-8 (NLT) But now Timothy has just returned, bringing us good news about your faith and love. He reports that you always remember our visit with joy and that you want to see us as much as we want to see you. So, we have been greatly encouraged in the midst of our troubles and suffering, dear brothers, and sisters, because you have remained strong in your faith. It gives us new life to know that you are standing firm in the Lord.

These verses show how much this letter of encouragement from Timothy lifted Paul's spirit. If Paul needed and appreciated an uplifting letter of encouragement how much more the small church leader of today. I once heard for every negative word spoken, we need 10 words of encouragement. This is a work greatly needed for our pastors today.

Mrs. Cheryl McDonnold
Sikeston, Missouri

For the pastor of a small church in a community of any size, discouragement seems to be lurking around every corner. When encouragement is hard to find, the desire to pack up the office and move on is very real. That is why this book needs to be within arm's reach of every small church pastor to find the strength to keep pressing forward. This collection of letters from one pastor to another just might be the inspiration you need in your work for the Lord.

Rev. Greg Perkins, Director
Church Development & Men's Ministries
Southern Missouri District Assemblies of God

Whatever your calling, it was placed in your heart by God Himself. In those times of doubt, remember our mission will not always be easy. Do not underestimate your influence on those around you and do not focus on your own idea of success. I am close friends with a few small-town pastors, and I am certain they underestimate their true impact on those around them. Take time to encourage these pastors, you may be the very reason they persevere. If you are a pastor, take one day at time, pray, and know that your community needs you.

Chief James B. McMillen
Director of Public Safety
Sikeston, Missouri

Before the pastor title, you have always been my dad first. You have always set your priorities to loving God first, family second, all people of all walks in life third, and never placing yourself, above any others. I have seen you struggle, cry, discouraged, frustrated, and hurt in the messiness entailed by ministry. I have only partially experienced the sacrifices you have made, because you always take care of others first. Your priority is humbly serving others like Jesus did. You have taught me to fight my battles in prayer and to place my faith in the hope only found in Jesus.

I have watched you help thousands and take no recognition. I have seen you work harder than anybody, and nobody sees it. I have seen you give your last dollar to somebody in need when it is literally all you had. When we had nothing, we prayed, had faith, and God always provided.

You have shown me that leadership is not about self-promotion but developing other leaders. It is not about getting things done in your timing, but having patience and letting God work in his timing. Your example and teaching have shown me that ministry is not about what I can do, but about how God uses the broken to bring him glory.

I have seen you get blindsided with unexpected life-threatening medical situations, false accusations, and I have heard you called every name in the book. You have shown me what it looks like to suffer for what is good. Despite the false slams and allegations, you have always kept your eyes on Jesus and fought on your knees in prayer. Despite life's unexpected circumstances, you have always fought on your knees in prayer. It is Jesus first, that is the real "secret." You have exemplified that being a pastor of a small church is not about gaining a spotlight. It is not about being the most talented, or even being the greatest speaker. The pastor of the small church is about compassion, selflessness, servanthood, obedience, and faithfulness unto the Lord. It is hard work and takes time. It is about planting seeds, patience, consistency, and learning to let go and let God. You have experienced both the pain and fruit of ministry. It is your experience and your story that I believe God will use to empower and encourage other small church pastors in their ministry.

Rev. Joshua McHaffie, Ministry Assistant
Impact Church
Ozark, MO

Dear Small Church Pastor,

This is not a how-to manual for growing a large thriving church, it is not ministry suggestions or a list of new ideas. However, it is a collection of heart-felt letters written to pastors of small towns and small churches who have been discouraged and have felt the earth under their feet let loose. This is a series of letters to encourage, lift up, and hopefully give pastors a much-needed reminder of their call to obedience.

Pastoring in small church or in a small town takes a big heart and lots of courage, with the ability to not take things personal and to pursue the high calling of God.

My suggestion for reading this book.

+ Do not read this book like a novel or any other chapter book you have ever read.
+ Simply read it like a letter that arrived in your mailbox today! Read one letter per day, or one letter per week, and realize the person sending this letter is your friend and co-laborer and has received many small-church battle scars too.

My wife, Susan, and I have been laboring in the ministry trenches for several years. I hope our family stories of faith, hope, joy, and perseverance will give you a spiritual lift and that you will be encouraged to share your stories of faith.

I have divided this book into 4 sections. These sections were created with my own blood, sweat, and tears in the hope of seeing God take these situations and use them for a greater good in the Kingdom of God. The section **Encouragement** is an obvious attempt to encourage church leaders. The section **Occupy** is personal stories where I wanted to give up, but I did not, and I got to witness God do the miraculous. **Obedience** is always the toughest section in life, but one of the most important. Stories of **Pain and Self-Care** are a huge part of my life and I would not trade those teaching moments for anything.

Please recognize this one thing, you are not alone, and we are better together!

Faithfully serving Jesus,

John McHaffie
Small Church Pastor

SECTION ONE

Encouragement

To give hope, faith & support

Dear Small Church Pastor,

I want to encourage you today!

I know you have read Social Media this week and you have heard about all the great things going on down the street at other churches ("the fastest growing church in the world," "Our programs are better than every other church," "Our events are da-bomb-dig-gety-yo," etc.) Here you are giving your best, fighting the good fight, preaching the Word, praying, and serving. Yet, your pews seem to not be filling as fast as church-folk say that they should. The well-meaning church-folk keep reminding you of the glory days when their church was amazing, their music was amazing, and the preaching was amazing.

But you know in your heart that the church you pastor is growing, slowly, but steadily. You are watching lives being drawn closer to Jesus through relationships and small groups.

I know, I know... Your board says you are low on funds and you need to increase the church tithes and offerings, as if you were running some kind of social business that you have control over volunteer giving.

BREATHE!!!

Remember, a mushroom will grow overnight, and it takes a lifetime to grow an oak tree. Not even windstorms have control over the great oak trees, but most mushrooms, which are fungus, can be uprooted easily!

Keep Growing, Keep Loving, Keep Nurturing and Keep Pastoring!

I support you, Pastor!

Faithfully Serving Jesus,

John McHaffie
Small Church Pastor

Dear Small Church Pastor,

I am writing this letter to encourage anyone pastoring a small church, whether it is rural, urban, suburban, church plant, or wherever God has called you. My language may seem like I am focusing only on Rural America. Why? Because that is where I am, it is what I know, who I have become, and some basic statistics show us that nearly 2/3 of most denominational churches are in Rural America.

If you are reading this and you are not rural, it is ok! Every pastor faces the same struggles and the same ole church-folk, same church boards, and the same nonsense. As they would say in the rural setting, simply, "Eat the meat and spit out the fat."

Rural Church Pastors are the fox-hole fighters, the front lines of the battle, yet many times they are the forgotten ones. Most urban and sub-urban settings have access to more technology, stores, people, money, and creative possibilities. Rural America will take a trip into "town" or "the city" and the whole family will get excited. In fact, many times you might even ask your neighbor if you need to pick anything up for them while you are "in town."

In rural America, some people have access to technology and others do not.

One church that I was privileged to pastor, at the north end of the town had access to wireless internet and the south end of town did not. I have lived in areas that had not embraced the wonderment wireless networks. In rural America, many people do not have the latest techno gadgets or toys, and most people do not know the difference, not because they are inferior, but because rural America has a different set of rules that they adhere to.

Rural Americans value family, friends, fishing, farming, school, church, and hunting as a way of life. Most conversations are not related to the newest phones, tablets, or computers, but possibly a gun, fishing pole, truck, or a new piece of farm machinery.

In rural America, most people have a technical degree in common sense from the School of Hard Knocks, and this is their education of choice. This is not to say small town people do not have college degrees, but most that have earned their college degree have done so with a special ingredient called hard work and determination.

The rural pastor is a man or woman who has given up opportunities to be in more affluent areas and due to their choice, they may not have the resources to hire a staff, manage large facilities, dress in fine clothes, drive a newer car, or brag about their new out-of-this-world sound and media system.

Rural pastors are possibly the hardest working people in the world. Perhaps, they are working a part-time job, mowing the church's 5-acre lot, while the spouse is cleaning the church facility as they are preparing for church tomorrow, and they cannot forget to pour the communion cups, clean the stain in the carpet, and visit Sister Bessie who has the shingles. There is an unwritten rule in all rural settings, you are encouraged to be at all community sporting events.

Rural pastors should be held up as spiritual heroes of the faith. They are God's gift to the church.

They are multi-task Extraordinaires.

I am hoping to encourage, uplift, humor, and honor all pastors. However, most of you are extremely busy and might not have time to read a book, but hopefully you will find time to read a letter from a co-laborer friend.

Faithfully Serving Jesus,

John McHaffie
Small Church Pastor

Dear Small Church Pastor,

There is a miracle in your house, but there may also be a miracle near your house.

God brought a miracle into my life as a gift. Rural Compassion a division of Convoy of Hope, has been contributing to struggling churches across this nation. Steve and Rebecca Donaldson obeyed God years ago when they established a ministry known as Rural Compassion that is addressing the heart felt needs of Rural America through...

- Resourcing. Providing food, shoes, and other supplies to churches and missionaries for distribution.
- Disaster Relief. Providing hands on assistance to rural areas during times of natural disaster; hurricanes, wildfires, tornadoes, floods, etc.
- Outreach. Providing training and hands-on help for large- and small-scale outreach.
- Public School Initiative. Helping churches become the best friend of the local schools.
- Pastoral Training. Developing cohorts of rural pastors or specialized training and support to develop the church as a resource center for the community.

Steve Donaldson says, "In the social world, 50 is the new 40, and 40 is the new 30. In the world of fashion and style, brown is the new black. In the world of ministry, Rural is the new inner city. For years, ministries have gone to the inner cities to reach hurting people. However, in the last few years, more people are realizing the dire needs in Rural America" (Convoy of Hope 2021).

When Steve came into my life as a ministry coach, mentor, and friend, I started seeing amazing results in our church. I am not talking about large numbers on Sunday morning or large donations in the offering plate. I am talking about the DNA of the local church began to change, to morph, like a caterpillar changing to a butterfly.

I started hearing church folk talk about our Shoe Outreaches, Book Fairs, Food distribution etc. The focus of the church's conversation did not seem to be in survival mode, past hurt or frustration. The eyes of the congregation started to look up! Do you not say, 'Four months more and then the harvest'? I tell you, open your eyes and look at the fields! They are ripe for harvest. John 4:35 (King James Bible 2021).

When we look up, we see Jesus. When we look up, we are not looking at each other, but our eyes are on the harvest and that makes Jesus smile.

Faithfully Serving Jesus,

John McHaffie
Small Church Pastor

Dear Small Church Pastor,

*I*f we take our eyes off Jesus and the harvest, we begin to look at each other. If we look at each other, we see imperfections, difference of opinions, color of skin, background, socio-economic positions, titles, etc. This is when we have church splits, committee failure, controlling spirits, and a host of other epidemics that only attempt to kill the church. So, open your eyes and look at the fields, they are ripe for the harvest. Look up!

When this little church of 48 people started looking at the fields and taking their eyes off each other, past hurts, and church splits began to dissipate. The healing among our people began to be evident, not only to the local church but within the community.

Convoy of Hope - Rural Compassion provided my church the necessary tools to reevaluate our mission, vision, and values. Periodically, we could do a bigger-than-life outreach with the help of other ministries in our region. The question is not, how big is my church? Rather, how much of an impact are we making on our community.

As we began to "Look up" at the fields some amazing things started to happen. Once again, this is not in the nickels and noses category, but in the mission, vision, and values. The least, the last and the lost began to matter to us as a church and the facility took a back seat in its value.

Everyone has their favorite time of the year, some like birthdays, first days of spring or Christmas. I have never heard anyone celebrate April 15th or IRS Day and for that matter the one day that is picked every year for your annual church business meeting.

I have heard horror stories about Annual Church Business Meetings; fist fights, yelling, screaming. I have never experienced these types of meetings, but as our church board and I were preparing for that meeting, I could only imagine that some of those things could be in my immediate future. Our annual finances were not necessarily that bad for the size of congregation, but we had a 57,339-square foot building to maintain. The facility was nearly 10 years behind in upkeep and items had depreciated in value to the point of total replacement.

We only had one option.

Sell the facility.

This facility was your standard rural church building. Everyone at some point had a part in the construction, kitchen, color, nursery, sheet rock, electric, concrete, plumbing... you get the point... To sell this facility meant we were selling everyone's memories, not only memories of the building process, but memories of baptisms, weddings, funerals, and mission services.

I knew in my heart what needed to be done, but... In one of my earlier letters, I was telling you that the apostle Paul and I are extremely different, and my personality is more like Barnabas. I knew this was God's plan, but I was unsure how God was going to pull this off.

First obstacle, the people!

Second obstacle, the facility itself!

Third obstacle, who would buy it!

The church membership did not object in the manner that I had prepared for in my mind. I was eager to find a backdoor and was beginning the process of "working myself out of a job," The church board prepared a professional power point presentation giving our congregation a choice in the matter with the idea of anyone having a better idea, we want to listen to you. On that Sunday, we agreed we should spend two weeks fasting and praying over the matter-at-hand and another meeting was scheduled two weeks later.

The next two weeks, I had a lot of homework. How do you sell a 57,339-square foot building that needs thousands of dollars' worth of upgrades? "Trust in the Lord with all your heart, lean not to your own understanding and in all your ways acknowledge him and he will make your paths straight" Proverbs 3:5-6 (King James Bible 2021).

That is how. You do not! If it is of God, He will!!!

God's will = God's bill.

Two weeks later the church membership voted and gave the church board permission to pursue looking for a buyer. We hired a realtor, and the process began. It was slow and for the most part unfruitful to say the least. We put our facility on the market for a 6-month contract and we did not get a hit until the fifth month and we were not completely satisfied with the proposed offer. We felt obligated to renegotiate a new price and we were able to accept the second offer.

SOLD!!!

We paid off all our outstanding debt on the facility and were able to lease the same facility/offices, nearly 9,000 square foot of space for 18 months with a $100.00 per month lease which included utilities.

Our goal was to take the money from the sale and build a facility that would be debt free and easy maintenance. It CAN be done!!!

Faithfully Serving Jesus,

John McHaffie
Small Church Pastor

Dear Small Church Pastor,

nonymity is not the most popular word in the American culture. Most of us put on a humble facade and sure, we do not like to talk in front of crowds or be the center of attention at a party, most of you do not like to be unknown. There are probably plenty of words that begin with the letter "A," but this is the one that tells my story.

For the most part, most of my adult ministry was pretty good. I had a pretty good run as a youth pastor and as a children's pastor. I felt like my wife and I were widely accepted among the churches that we served. My dry humor and slightly sarcastic personality were usually characterized as an easy-to-get-along with, a basic nice guy. I never had any enemies that I was aware of and I felt confident about my abilities and gifts as an ordained minister of the gospel.

I know God had a plan for me before the foundations of the world. I like to think that God had a picture of me on his refrigerator while he was saying, "Let there be light."

So, here I am, married... kids... dream job... college degree... ordained...

However, I had never experienced being broken.

Hard Knock U was about to be in session. The registration line for HKU was forming, and I was waiting to become a student of the most difficult school in the world. I am a firm believer that you are not worth your salt in ministry until you have been broken.

There is nothing more that I like to do on a cold wintery Sunday afternoon than to watch a classic western movie. I love the horses, gun fights, spitting, bar fights, hangings, and there is always a jail break. In most westerns, horses are the main mode of transportation for everyone. However, horses do not just "high-ho-silver" naturally.

In the Wild West, horses were not domesticated animals, there was a process of breaking the horse of its wild and crazy ways. Wild horses were free to roam the plains and go to-and-fro, whenever they pleased. These wild horses were of great value to the development of America's Wild West and many of these beautiful stallions had to be broken before they could be useful to the rider.

I was not wild in the sense of worldliness, but wild in the understanding that I was God's gift to the church, and I had this "ministry thing" all figured out.

I had recently served on staff at a great church in Illinois, a church known for its missions giving, powerful youth group, amazing children's ministry, and a deep passion for the deeper things of God. But... it was time for me to go back to school... Not seminary, but the proverbial Hard Knock U.

The U-Haul was loaded, and we are off! "Woo-hoo," I thought, "I'm no longer the staff person, I'm the Senior pastor, I'm the boss..."

A few days later I walked out of my parsonage and said, "Dear Lord, what have I done?"

I stood on my porch and stared at the building across the parking lot and wondered if I was qualified for this new assignment.

I enter the office and I am greeted by the staff and at that point I felt pretty good. I felt important for nearly 2 years. Then, it happened. I started hearing stories that I was not loved and adored by some of the church folk. This was devastating to my delicate little psyche. This was a new feeling to me. I did not like it, not at all. So, I did what anyone would do. I tried harder to make people like me.

This was not working either. So, I did what anyone else would do, I went home and buried my head in my pillow and cried like a baby and asked God to remove me from my infirmity... "God, these people don't like me!!"

I blamed it on the weather, I blamed it on the culture, I blamed it on their poor discipleship classes, I blamed it on former pastors, I blamed it on the board, and I blamed it on everyone but myself.

My new assignment was the classic run-down church with immediate need of revitalization and renewal. A decade ago, this church was running several hundred and now it was under 100 people on Sunday morning. However, it still had the same bills to pay, as it had for a decade. I was told by different pastors that I had taken a "tiger by the tail." One pastor asked me what I needed to prove by accepting this pastorate at this church. Needless to say, this assignment was a colossal challenge. Multiple staff, small budget, and big bills.

God began to show me how to navigate through these treacherous waters of uncertainty. This job was not going to be easy, but it was possible. Surrounding me was a great group of board members who loved God with all their heart and wanted to see this church built up for God's glory. They began to pray with me, and a divine plan was devised...

Little did I know, school was now in session.

It was hard for me to believe that church people did not like me or trust me. I had to make a very unpopular decision with the church staff and ask them to resign or accept the current leadership's vision and values. They left the church! Plain and simple.

I cried! I cried like a baby all Sunday afternoon.

I had never felt that kind of pain before in ministry. I could not blame it on my senior pastor or anyone else. This was my situation to deal with, whether I liked it or not.

I was starting to feel as though I was not God's gift to the ministry. I challenged God daily to "take this cup from me." I wanted out. I hated ministry People were hurting my feelings. This is not fair. I went to an opposite approach to ministry. I felt I could not do anything right; tons of self-pity raged through my heart. It was time to quit. If I could not be well liked, loved, and appreciated then it was time to leave.

All that experience had diluted down to nothing and I was able to move on with my life and ministry. This church could have easily been renamed, "That 70's Church." You can imagine the burnt orange carpet, burnt orange pews and deep dark brown tones complimenting this ocean of orange. A hot water heater was the main decoration in the main church lobby, adorned with its broken dated-tile and yellowed ceiling tiles.

In the fellowship hall the main color was purple. Yes, you heard correctly the two dominant colors of our facility were orange and purple complimented by dark chocolate brown tones. After members of our staff had been asked to resign, two years later our bank account was strong, and we decided to remodel the interior and with great success. This job was completed on time or target and under budget.

Nearing the end of this project, more people started stirring up more false accusations that had to be dealt with. This type of behavior is never an easy thing to deal with, but I was more prepared for the next round of rough waters than I had ever been in my life. One day in prayer, God spoke into my spirit and said, "Never go to war, but always go to worship." I had learned to rely on God to fight my battles, as I simply went into a season of worship.

The biggest lesson I learned during that battle was that I had to rely on God in the ministry!

When I was amid trouble, God could use me more when I depended on him! During this season of brokenness, I received more from God in my quiet times than I had ever experienced in my life. I felt blessed to have gone through those trials and it was during that season God was preparing me for what I am doing to this day.

My time of ministry had come to an end at this particular church. It was bitter-sweet, yet I was ready to move on and see what adventures God had for me and my family.

As I began this process, once again I was not being obedient to my calling to obedience.

I kept sending resumes to numerous great churches, bigger cities, and more affluent communities. I sent out countless resumes, CD's, portfolios and never received as much as a rejection letter in return. My heart kept pointing me to this one little quaint city in southwest Missouri, as I kept telling my heart to be quiet. This little community consumed my free time. I looked at every demographic, web site, and article about southwest Missouri I could find, my curiosity piqued as I knew this was where God was sending my family.

My biggest problem once again was myself. I thought I deserved a bigger, better position in exchange for all the pain I had encountered. God spoke to me so clear one day while I was in prayer, and asked me, "Are you willing to go somewhere and be unknown? Are you willing to serve me without any recognition from your peers?"

Unfortunately, I struggled with that question. I should have been able to answer that easily. However, I still had an unhealthy level of "selfishness" dominating my obedience.

Over the next couple of weeks, I spent a lot of time fasting and in prayer while struggling with the thought of total isolation and anonymity. Being anonymous was not on my agenda, but God was working through some details in my life that allowed my will to be broken in a powerful way.

Jesus said, "If you lift me higher, I will draw all men unto me."

Are you willing to serve in places where your fame will not be great, and you seem to have no way to climb any ladders of success?

I pray that you will be challenged to be obedient to the call of God on your life. Even if you must give up your pride and serve in the middle of nowhere.

Anonymity may seem scary, unfruitful, and unrealistic in ministry, but I challenge you to make Jesus famous and do not worry about your position, title, entitlements, or any other thing that takes the glory from Jesus. Just Jesus.

Faithfully Serving Jesus,

John McHaffie
Small Church Pastor

Dear Small Church Pastor,

Sometimes we all may feel as though we have been banished to the isle of Patmos.

The Isle of Patmos was a small island with its main purpose being isolation for those sentenced to life in prison. More than likely, Patmos was a mining island that used prisoners as slave labor during the Roman Empire. John had a much different experience when he was banished to the isle of Patmos than his fellow prisoners. He experienced one of the greatest revival services ever attended by anyone in the Bible and was only attended by John and Jesus on the isle of Patmos! Jesus said, "Come up higher…"

Desire His presence and not the adoration of men!

Serve him with faithfulness, obedience, and complete surrender. You might feel isolated, but you are never alone. God said, "I will never leave you or forsake you; I am with you until the end of the age."

If you feel you are all alone.

Listen.

Can you hear Him, saying, "Come up higher."

Faithfully Serving Jesus,

John McHaffie
Small Church Pastor

Dear Small Church Pastor:

*W*hen we first moved to this little southwest Missouri town, I was not prepared to purchase a home. We rented a beautiful farmhouse on a 3-acre lot for one year. We had been living in a major city, on a major highway, in a church parsonage that was located in the church parking lot for the past seven years, and now I am standing at my front door holding a steaming hot cup of coffee in my hand while the only thing I can see in front of me is a dozen or more cows standing in a plush green field and those beautiful bovines never seemed to care what I was doing. It was refreshing! Rolling hills, farm animals, ponds, and the overwhelming smell of nature. As I worked daily on my 3-acre lawn, I began to take notice of the natural elements all around me.

During the process of selling our church facility, building a new facility, and all the other changes, I started watching and learning about the behavior of the butterfly. A butterfly is simply amazing! It starts off as a slimy little worm and then, BOOM! It turns into this bright colorful butterfly that can fly thousands of miles.

The worm's instincts say, "It's time to build a cocoon." Up until that point I am not sure the worm even knew what a cocoon was. Now, he is building one to live in. So, he winds and winds the threadlike string around his whole body and once completely covered something amazing called metamorphosis begins to happen... His DNA begins to change, and his future will be utterly different from his past. He will learn to eat differently. His mode of transportation will be his wings, and everyone will see him in a different light and not remember his past. "He makes all things new."

This newly found enlightenment made me realize that most of our churches Need to go through a metamorphic state. I really believe God wants to turn some of our wormy churches into bright and beautiful butterflies, but we must be willing to go through the metamorphic state of waiting on God, not getting in a hurry, being patient with the process and watching and seeing what happens.

However, during the process, if the worm's cocoon gets damaged too early, or decides not to break out, the butterfly will not fly. It is all in perfect timing. Be patient with the process. Do not try to be make things happen too early. Wait on God! Enjoy the process. One day every wormy church will crawl out of its dirty little cocoon and fly!!!

The church needs to fly again!

It was time to put on my boots, grab some gloves and get to work.

Faithfully Serving Jesus,

John McHaffie
Small Church Pastor

Dear Small Church Pastor,

I heard a joke a few years ago while I was a children's pastor. Why do geese fly in a V formation? Because it would be too hard for geese to fly in an E formation! I apologize for that joke, and I am pretty sure you it will not be in your next sermon.

In a You Tube video called *A Great lesson from Geese in the V-Formation* (Pacitti 2015)- I was enlightened to learn why geese fly in the V-formation flight pattern when migrating to more southern regions, this v-formation serves two important purposes in the flight of the geese:

First, it preserves their energy. Each bird flies slightly above the bird in front of him, resulting in a reduction of wind resistance. The birds take turns being the leader in front, falling back when they get tired. The geese can fly for a long period of time before they rest. Wow, stop and think about that! Selah!

The second reason geese fly in the V-formation, it is much easier to keep track of every bird in the group. Flying in the v-formation helps with communication and coordination of their journey.

This is powerful imagery of GEESE. All of them are leaders. All of them are heading to the same destination. All of them have each other's back. All of them win.

If the church would develop a V-Formation in its leadership models, we might see the church fly higher and longer than it has ever flown, and the church might be able to enjoy the view for a moment and enjoy the ride.

Faithfully Serving Christ,
John McHaffie
Small Church Pastor

Dear Small Church Pastor,

O ne of the greatest weapons used to destroy ministers is not as obvious as one could imagine.

When you think of a minister being in a spiritual battle this usually brings up mental images of sexual misconduct, financial misconduct, or trouble in their marriage or family. I am not trying to say these issues do not exist; however, this is not the greatest threat against the church around the world. The biggest weapon, in my opinion, is discouragement. The Bible says, "The enemy comes to kill, steal, and destroy."

Nehemiah 2: 11;12, "Nevertheless, my journey continued until I reached Jerusalem. After three days in the city, under the cover of darkness, I was accompanied by a small group of men. The True God had placed a secret plan on my heart, and there I had left it hidden until the time was right. No one knew what it was I imagined for Jerusalem" (Nelson 2012).

This can be one of the loneliest feelings you can experience on this planet. In these situations, you seem to lose your will to carry on, you find little purpose in your existence, you begin to rationally pick yourself apart and convince yourself that you are not of any value to anyone, to God or to the ministry.

Satan is deceptive! He is busy stealing, killing, and destroying and would love to demolish your hopes and dreams. He never rests, he never breaks down and he never stops for any reason. Why is Satan so busy doing this? He lives to oppose God and destroy your God-Given purpose! He fights every purpose and plan in your life in hopes that you will give up, stop, and forsake your divine purpose and calling.

In these times, I have to go to the scripture and breathe the words of life over my circumstances. In these times, I must tell the enemy that I am not a quitter. I must remind myself that God is my source, my strength, and I am not afraid for *no weapon formed against me will prosper.*

I would like to reflect on a day in the life of Nehemiah. He was a committed follower that needed to finish a God-Given task, a man who was drawn to the will of God and his testimony reflected his actions and values.

Nehemiah was no stranger to opposition. As soon as Nehemiah took his first step toward his God-given great goal, his troubles began.

> Nehemiah 2:10 "When Sanballat the Horonite, and Tobiah the servant, the Ammonite, heard of it, it grieved them exceedingly that there was come a man to seek the welfare of the children of Israel" (King James Bible 2021).

It seems like the enemy always finds some willing vessel to do his work. It may be someone you know but does not understand your God-Given vision or it might be someone in authority who wants nothing to do with this vision. Nonetheless, the enemy will find someone to throw a discouraging rock at you and your God-Given Vision.

When Nehemiah announced the plan for the rebuilding of the walls, he forged forward with courage and purpose as more and more trouble came at him.

> Nehemiah 2:19 "But when Sanballat the Horonite, and Tobiah the servant, the Ammonite, and

Geshem the Arabian, heard it, they laughed us
to scorn, and despised us, and said, 'What is this
thing that ye do? will ye rebel against the king'"
(King James Bible 2021)?

The trouble did not end until after the job was completed. Any movement forward for God will result in some type of opposition. The fact of the matter is, we should not be startled by this behavior, and this behavior is one of the oldest tricks in the enemy's playbook. Dealing with the opposition is never, I repeat never, a sign that you are out of the will and purpose of God. On the contrary, it is usually evidence that you are heading in the correct direction and this makes our little enemy a bit scared and nervous when we refuse to back down.

How do you know what the opposition looks like? In this case, you have Governor Sanballat of Samaria who was related to many Jews, Tobiah, this is a Jewish name, more than likely was a renegade Jew that was the Governor's aid, and Geshem, the governor's secret service agent who served him as a hired gun.

These three men were citizens of that region, who lived in close proximity to the Jews and did not have a good reason to cause trouble, but most of the time opposition came from people who should not be causing it.

The motivation behind this opposition is basic in its development.

- <u>Selfish</u> people live in the present and love to see others fail so they can gloat about how "right" they were concerning their opinions.
- <u>Jealousy</u> does not like others to win or even have a good idea; jealous people live in the past and compare everything

to yesterday and how we have always done it. New ideas can cause opposition to their past successes.

- <u>Bitterness</u> lives in their future because of an issue that has happened in the past. Bitterness is a choice you choose to carry. Bitterness will never lead you to a spirit empowered lifestyle.

As we see in the book of Nehemiah, some things never change. The source of our opposition comes from the enemy of our soul who kills, steals, and destroys. His tactics have not changed since the Garden of Eden, "Lust of the flesh, the lust of the eyes and the pride of life." Unfortunately, his tactics seem to be as effective today as they were in the beginning.

What can we learn from the opposition? When we are faced with difficulty in our lives, difficult people in our lives, we tend to default to a retreat mode. Nehemiah knew that his orders were from the Lord and that this mission was bathed in prayer.

Nehemiah 1:5-10 - And said, I beseech thee, O Lord God of heaven, the great and terrible God, that keepeth covenant and mercy for them that love him and observe his commandments: Let thine ear now be attentive, and thine eyes open, that thou mayest hear the prayer of thy servant, which I pray before thee now, day and night, for the children of Israel thy servants, and confess the sins of the children of Israel, which we have sinned against thee: both I and my father's house have sinned. We have dealt very corruptly against thee, and have not kept the commandments, nor the statutes, nor the judgments, which thou commandedst thy servant

Moses. Remember, I beseech thee, the word that thou commandedst thy servant Moses, saying, If ye transgress, I will scatter you abroad among the nations: But if ye turn unto me, and keep my commandments, and do them; though there were of you cast out unto the uttermost part of the heaven, yet will I gather them from thence, and will bring them unto the place that I have chosen to set my name there. Now these are thy servants and thy people, whom thou hast redeemed by thy great power, and by thy strong hand (King James Bible 2021).

Nehemiah 2:18 - Then I told them of the hand of my God which was good upon me; as also the king's words that he had spoken unto me. And they said, let us rise up and build. So, they strengthened their hands for this good work (King James Bible 2021). Nehemiah had a divine confirmation that was a vision from God, and not from a selfish or prideful desire to rebuild the walls of the city.

Nehemiah 2:8 – "And the king granted me, according to the good hand of my God upon me." In Nehemiah chapter two we are given a divine playbook on how to respond when opposition arises (King James Bible 2021).

+ His purpose was firm, his trust was in God, and no one could take his eyes off the goal of rebuilding the walls of that city.
+ He prayed for guidance and gave praise to God for this mission.
+ He kept the plan in front of the people.
+ He refused to give up any land and
+ He claimed this territory for the Lord's glory.
+ He protected his God-given mission by refusing to be a people pleaser; he refused to give honor to his opponents.

Have you ever started something for God, but immediately opposition arose?

If so, you must allow that the God-Given great goal to generate purpose in your life. This is not the time to quit, get an attitude, get bitter or lose heart. This is the time for you to reevaluate what you are doing and reaffirm the role that God has in this situation. Recommit to sticking with the God-Given great goal that God has placed in your heart.

If the cousins of Tobiah and Sanballet are members in your church, stick with the goal no matter what the opposition says. God is greater!

Here is an equation I learned many years ago: $2+2=4$ but, $2+2+God = $ a whole lot more

If God is on your side, then who can be against you?

Lead on! Fight on! God is with you!

Faithfully Serving Christ,

John McHaffie
Small Church Pastor

Dear Small Church Pastor,

*H*ere are a few questions I would love to discuss with you at length, over a cup of hot coffee and with a few of our close friends. Some of these questions are mine in thought and intent, and others are from other sources that I have not yet been able to wrap my heart around and form an opinion that I am satisfied.

I pray that we can keep our communications open, full of the spirit and full of grace and truth as we plod on, plod on, plod on.

1. What is the difference between SERVING our Community and ENABLING our community?
2. How can we develop a "local mission's strategy" to help transform rural communities? Are we using the Acts 1:8 missions' model, Neighborhoods to Nations?
3. Do we own the lostness of our community?
4. Do we own the pain of our community?
5. Do we own the brokenness in our community?
6. Do we care about our city or our "holier than thou" reputation in our city?
7. Do we see our church setting as part of the greater global initiative for world missions?

My hope is that you will desire a burden for our communities around the nation.

Maybe you are a pastor of a thriving church, would you adopt a small church pastor and family and help them fulfill their calling?

Maybe you are a college student looking for your big break. Look no further than Rural America. I beg you, do not use this for a catapult to a better, more comfortable position. Plant yourself! Take your time! Enjoy the journey as you build a marvelous ministry.

Maybe you are not sure what to do… Take a drive deep into the country and pray for direction! Ask God if this is possibly your destiny!

You have permission to quote my buddy, Al Hillberg, "*It CAN be done!*"

Faithfully Serving Jesus,

John McHaffie
Small Church Pastor

Dear Small Church Pastor,

I am writing this letter as I am dealing with COVID-19 and online church. Do not let social media pressures and social media comparisons distract you from your high calling. You have been called to lead in the city that you pastor by God Himself. He chose you *"for such a time as this."*

You might not have the biggest, baddest, latest, greatest audio/video tools to get your church service online. Yes, there are churches that have the capability of a high-quality television studio-like service. But remember, you are not called to impress, out-do, or become a cool internet star. You are called to pastor, you are a shepherd, you are leading your congregation through the most troubling times of their lives.

It is rather simple. Be you! Be real! Be Jesus!

Connect with your congregation over the internet but do not be tempted to fall into the trap of comparing your church to other churches and ministries. Do not worry about the stuff that is out of your control.

No one expects a TBN, CBN or Daystar production from you.

Our church people need to know that God still sits on the throne, that you are praying, and that we are better together.

I totally understand your struggle. Even today, I am wrestling with preaching a bit differently, I am wrestling with content, I am wrestling with equipment, I am wrestling with a low-budget, I am wrestling with the same stuff that you are wrestling with.

Let us make a commitment right now!

This Sunday, Wednesday, or weekday, let us give our congregations our best, pray for our cities, pray for our churches, and fight the good fight of faith. Meanwhile, call people, deliver food, mow a yard, fix a fence, give blood, volunteer, check on the elderly, and rest!

We might be in this for a while, so saddle up and let us blaze this wild, uncharted region of the Church Online Media frontier together and pray that God gives us favor, new creativity, bigger media budgets and that He uses us in new ways and the Kingdom of God will be greater by us living in complete obedience to Jesus.

Faithfully Serving Jesus,

John McHaffie
Small Church Pastor

Dear Small Church Pastor,

There seems to be a great paradox in the world of the professional clergy.

Obviously, we all feel called, or we would find a new vocation. Am I right?

Our profession takes a toll on our self-esteem, family, friends, and for the most part we have never had a weekend off to go to the lake, beach, or the river.

The paradox is difficult to handle and goes like this: You have found favor in the local school, your county, your city, your police, and sheriff's office. You have become a stakeholder, and shared at Rotary, Lions, Kiwanis, and any other service club in your city. However, even though you have found favor in those areas, you have never felt as though you have found favor with the church that God placed you to serve.

Crazy thought, right?

Have you ever felt this way?

I will never be good enough for my church people!

+ I worship, but I use the wrong style of music.
+ I pray, but not as powerfully as former pastors.
+ I preach, but never as good as past preachers.
+ I serve, but I go to the wrong people.
+ I develop relationships, but to the wrong people.
+ I lead, but in their eyes, the wrong direction.

Pastors let me encourage your soul.

The good news is this, we were never called to be man pleasers. Only God pleasers.

Preach your best, pray your hardest, love everyone, serve with your gifts, build deep relationships, continue to worship the Lord with everything.

I pray that God would encourage you to draw closer to him and that you will be super-naturally recharged for the great task of leading your community to Jesus.

Small Church Pastor, you are amazing, and your community and church are blessed to have you.

Wise words of an old preacher and former professor... "Plod on! Plod on! Plod on!"

Faithfully serving Jesus,

John McHaffie
Small Church Pastor

Dear Small Church Pastor,

$\mathcal{S}$everal pastors have requested resources and tools for building a strong, vibrant, healthy church community.

- Newspaper Archives
- Chamber of Commerce
- EDC – Economic Development Committee
- City Hall
- Court House
- Hospitals
- Past Community Assessments
- Local Library
- School System
- University or Extension Office
- Surveys
- Websites

  - www.census.gov
  - County websites
  - State Websites
  - www.thearda.com
  - www.epodunk.com
  - www.dataplace.org

Resources for Rural Pastors

1. Church of Irresistible Influence – Robert Lewis
2. Helping Public Schools – Jim Schmidt
3. Externally Focused Church – Eric Swanson

4. 101 Ways to Reach Your Community – Steve Sjogren
5. The Circle Maker – Mark Batterson
6. Transforming Church in Rural America – Shannon O'Dell

Outreaches Developed for Rural Churches

1. Meet with your community stake holders – Be intentional in developing solid relationships with your community leaders.
2. Public School Involvement – Be the best friend of your school system.
3. Adoption Program – Adopt a community service provider/school staff/fireman/police, etc.
4. Community Special Event Involvement – Be intentional in being involved in your community's special events.
5. Shoes/School Supplies – Convoy of Hope - Rural Compassion could help resource your church by providing shoes or school supplies for your community. However, there is an application process, a fee and a waiting list for this program, for more information you can go to www.ruralcompassion.org
6. Food Pantry/Clothing Closet/Thrift Store Ministry – Offer your community help by providing food and clothing.
7. Bible Distribution – Give community volunteers and employees like Fireman, policeman and golfers a personized Bible.
8. Helping Hands Ministry – Designate a group in your church to be 100 percent committed to finding ways to serve your community. www.outreachmagizine.com
9. CERT Training – CERT is the Community Emergency Response Teams and offers free training that will certify

member of your church to be disaster relief responders and
providers. www.citizencorps.gov/cert

10. Offer "Need Based" Programs – Celebrate Recovery,
    MOPS, Financial Peace, Fireproof Marriage Training

11. Get involved with your Special Needs community. For
    example: Night to Shine sponsored by Tim Tebow
    Foundation.

12. Talk with the Fire Chief, Chief of Police, and wrestle with
    the idea of starting a chaplaincy program.

You will be surprised by the support you will get from locals
once you connect your compassionate heart with their compassionate heart and watch the sparks fly as you work together to build
the Kingdom of God.

Faithfully Serving Jesus,

John McHaffie
Small Church Pastor

Dear Small Church Pastor,

$\mathcal{S}$tay true to your calling. Stay true to your first love. Stay true to obedience. Stay true to Jesus.

In John 15, Jesus is preparing his disciples for His departure, by way of death. He instructs them about their God-given calling and mission to fulfill as followers of Jesus. In verse five, Jesus creates this amazing and contemporary word picture the disciples to understand the importance of this moment. "I am the vine; you are the branches. If you remain in me and I in you, you will bear much fruit; apart from me you can do nothing" (King James Bible 2021).

The vine is Jesus! We are the branches. God the Father is the gardener. The gardener gently and methodically prunes the branches, for one reason or another, but primarily to bear more fruit.

The Gardener throws away the unfruitful branches into the fire for they have become useless to the garden.

One thing is clear in John 15, we must "abide" in the vine. We are to remain faithful by our personal devotion and pray regularly. If we abide in Him, the mutual nature of this covenant is He who will remain in us, forever. However, if we have no devotion to Him, no prayer life, no interaction with Him at all, there will be no fruit and we will be cast away. When you remain in Christ, you are dependent on Him. Have you ever noticed, a branch is dependent on the vine, but the vine is not dependent on the branch for life? Once again, the branch is useless without the vine. We need Jesus and more of him daily. The words "abide," "remain" and "stay" are three words that should motivate us to bloom where we are planted and trust in Jesus for the next step, no matter hard or difficult the situation may be.

Your personal devotional life is more than reading from a popular journal, memes, bible apps, or a devotional book. Your devotion to Christ is based on your obedience to abide in the vine, to remain in him, to stay close to the heart of the Father.

Simply keep the words of Jesus close to your heart, soul, and mind. Be renewed daily, which will revive your spirit to shape you, sanctify you, fill you and form you to become one who bears much fruit.

Stay close to Jesus!

Faithfully Serving Jesus,

John McHaffie
Small Church Pastor

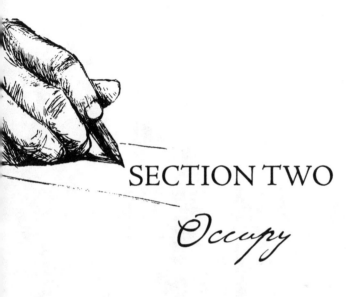

SECTION TWO

Occupy

To walk aggressively and faithfully into your divine calling.

Dear Small Church Pastor,

*H*ave you ever wanted to quit?

Has your ministry heart stopped beating as powerfully as it used to beat? Is your energy incrementally getting lower? Is your ministry drive slowing down? Have you lost the pep in your step or zip in your trip?

If you have any of these symptoms, you are in need SHEE-P-R.

What is SHEE-P-R? It is a life-giving procedure to help pastors stimulate their unresponsive heart for ministry, so it will start pumping powerfully again.

As you know, CPR is Cardiopulmonary resuscitation, which is an emergency procedure that combines chest compressions and sometimes the use of artificial ventilation with the hope to manually preserve the brain function to restore blood flow.

Also, QPR is a gatekeeper class you can take to help someone who is considering self-harm or suicide. Question, Persuade, and Refer.

SHEE-P-R, on the other hand, is for pastors when the sheep have worn you out and you are ready to run, quit and contemplate leaving the ministry.

I know that you have read the story where Jesus was willing to leave the 99 sheep to save the one, but you wish you could load your sheep onto a livestock trailer and sell them at the local stock yard. When you feel this way, you need SHEE-P-R.

Symptoms:

- You feel guilty because you want to quit.
- You feel ashamed because you are burned out.

- You do not remember the last time you prayed.
- You do not have a Bible Study plan.
- You seem more vulnerable toward worldly issues.
- You walk into your sanctuary and board meetings with your tail between your legs.
- You feel like this is your last pastorate.

I will address some ministry statistics in my next letter to you.

Faithfully Serving Jesus,

John McHaffie
Small Church Pastor

Dear Small Church Pastor,

Have you ever heard this statistic, "87% of all statistics are made up?"

It is a statement that is meant for you to, hopefully Laugh Out Loud - and not for serious conversation. Most pastors have used this quote in a sermon or at least laughed when they have heard it stated. When it comes to statistics, we tend to shy away from hard data that portrays our local ministry to being non-effective, unsuccessful, or uninteresting.

You work hard, you pray hard, and you live out the great commission the best you can in your assigned areas. One statistic that I have heard from a variety of resources over the years is that roughly 1,500 ministers leave the ministry every month. I have seen higher numbers and I have seen lower numbers in correlation with this statistic.

To me, this statistical number is not what is important, but YOU are!

If one person gets discouraged, defeated, and wants to leave the ministry, that my friend is the real tragedy.

I hope through these pages your focus will become clearer, your stamina will become stronger, and that you will be able to say with Winston Churchill, "Never give in, never give in, never, never, never, never—in nothing, great or small, large or petty—never give in except to convictions of honor and good sense" (Israel 2013).

Faithfully Serving Jesus,

John McHaffie
Small Church Pastor

Dear Small Church Pastor,

I suppose all of us at some time or another have been discouraged and wanted to give up and quit. In the heat of the struggle we will say, "I'll leave this church! Then, they will miss me. They'll wish they had been nicer to me and my family!" This is a dangerous place to live, at the corner of Offended and Hurt. You are basing your ministry value on what church-folk think about you. Move away from this intersection, because it is way too dangerous. Take a deep breath… Breathe deeply. Yes, that breath was a gift, God has given you breath, hope, and purpose.

We often struggle with feelings of inferiority of not meeting up to the unrealistic expectations put on us by church-folk and our church boards. We say:

- There is no use.
- The harder I try, the worse my situation gets.
- I am just spinning my wheels on the treadmill of church life.
- I am not getting anything completed on the church life do-do-list.
- I am a mess!
- I am confused!

Today, you must wrap your arms around this thought, 'Quitting is not an option.'

In your Bible you have lists and lists of men and women who have been tempted to give up and quit. They felt unqualified to finish was God called them to do. I would like to show you a few examples of these men and women who did not quit, but got extremely close to quitting:

Moses – In most theological circles Moses would be considered one of the greatest leaders who ever lived. Moses had God's power on his life, but in Numbers 11:15 he said to God, "If this is how you are going to treat me, please go ahead and kill me—if I have found favor in your eyes—and do not let me face my own ruin" (King James Bible 2021).

Joshua – During this era, you would not be stretching the truth to say that Joshua was the greatest biblical general. The beginning of the book of Joshua it says, "Moses my servant is dead" (King James Bible 2021). General Joshua gets promoted to the leader of the Hebrews. Joshua was handpicked by God to lead Israel into the Promised Land, but in Joshua 7:7, "If only we had been content to stay on the other side of the Jordan" (King James Bible 2021)! — He said "So… this is what we get for serving God" (King James Bible 2021)? Joshua had experienced the crossing of the Jordan, the unprecedented defeat of Jericho and now he felt like quitting!

Elijah – If it were left up to me, I would highly consider Elijah as the greatest prophet in Old Testament. He confronted a problem of that day, idolatry. He was the first prophet to trash talk the prophets of Baal and he won the face-off that day. He shouted at them, mocked them, and ultimately had them killed. Elijah called fire down from Heaven, which was an embarrassing blow to the Baal Boys on that day. As you read on, Elijah ran faster than King Ahab's chariot, most of us would consider that a successful day.

When you turn the pages of your Bible to 1 Kings 19:4, Elijah wanted to die, and said, God, take my life from me! "While he himself went a day's journey into the wilderness. He came to a broom bush, sat down under it, and prayed that he might die. 'I have had enough, Lord,' he said. 'Take my life; I am no better than my ancestors'" (King James Bible 2021).

Job – When we talk about Job we are reminded of his patience and faith, and that he was a great man. Job had a great beginning and a great ending, but the in-between years are a little sketchy. He lost everything and wished that he had never been born. Job became suicidal and extremely depressed for a long period of time! In Job 3:3 he said, "Let the day perish in which I was born" (King James Bible 2021).

Jonah - He wanted God to kill him because he was spiritually depressed and not even concerned for the all the souls that just got saved in Nineveh! This may have been one of the most powerful revival services in the history of our Judeo-Christian heritage. Jonah is tasked with the mission of going to the meanest, most worldly city in the modern world and confront them with their sins, calling them to repentance. Jonah finally responds to God in obedience and revival falls, but Jonah simply wants to die like the vine he is sitting under.

Paul - In Acts 18 we find Paul in his 2nd missionary journey, arriving from Athens to Corinth experiencing a low time in his life, a possible bout with depression. The great Apostle Paul, that week had walked 53 miles from Berea to Athens. The apostle was not received in Thessalonica. Trouble had ensued in Berea, and now he is in Athens, where it seems as though there is a god for every resident.

You & I – I am fully aware that we are not bible characters but let us pretend for a moment that the Bible was still being written today and we got added to the rag-a-muffin cast that make the story of the bible so real.

Go back into the secret place of your mind and recall the time you asked God to take you out of the ministry battle! "God, I've had enough! This pastoring thing is not what I bargained for." You are guilty, as am I of questioning God and his divine plan and purpose for your life, community, church, and your family.

Faithfully Serving Jesus,

John McHaffie
Small Church Pastor

Dear Small Church Pastor,

*O*ut of curiosity, have you ever wondered if questioning God is wrong?

When I am alone with God, in that personal, safe daily devotion zone, I seem to display the behavior of a preschool child who is in the company of his loving parents, innocent questions, transparent motives with complete safety, and trust. "Daddy, why is the grass green? Why do Zebras have stripes? Why is the sky blue? Why? Why? Why?"

Questions are basic learning tools we acquire at a young age. Questions are how we get answers. We are taught that questions are never wrong to ask.

I know you have heard the phrase that there is no such thing as a stupid question. However, most of us ignore the HUGE elephant in the room in our quiet time and we seem to never ask God, WHY? If I asked God this question, he might get offended, become annoyed at me, or reprimand me for not having enough faith.

So, as a pastor of a small church, you more-than-likely feel like you live in an isolated bubble, you experience loneliness every day, and insecurity seems to be your spiritual gift. For you, suffering has become a natural part of your life and you feel ashamed to ask such embarrassing questions.

So, I will attempt to ask these questions for you:

- Why do I want to quit?
- Why do other pastors seem to be more successful than me?
- Why do other pastors seem to not have financial issues like mine?
- Why can't I afford to have two nice cars?

- Why do I have to be here?
- Why can't I go minister somewhere better?
- Is there something wrong with me?
- Do I have what it takes?
- Will I ever be successful in ministry?
- Why can't we afford to go on mission's trips?
- Why do I have to feel so lonely?
- Why did God place me on the Isle of Patmos?
- Did I do something wrong to end up here?
- When will I be able to get the latest smart phone?
- Why do I have to use this old computer?
- Why, Lord?

These are simple questions that perhaps have been haunting you for years.

The questions of "why" can stir the hearts, emotions, and imaginations of the young and old alike, as it has been doing for generations.

- Why do turnips and beets exist?
- Why does Murphy's Law tend to resemble my personal life?
- Why does cancer exist?
- Why does the government tell lies?
- Why are there faithful Cub fans?
- Why can't I pastor a successful church?

The BIG "why" question in my life is this... "Why Me?"

Why did God choose and call this socially awkward man into vocational, full-time ministry? Why would God entrust to me the story of His plan of salvation for people in a modern-day era? Why?

As you are reading this letter, please remember that I am not a professional writer, articulate or renowned speaker, and I do not feel like that I have any new stately advice for you. I too, am a work in progress when it comes to church administration, outreach, and evangelism. In many ways, I am just like you.

However, I see many pastors who seem to have the golden Midas touch on ministry and personal success stories that seem to lead their way. Praise God for their ability to lead, grow and create an awesome ministry environment, but I must be transparent with you, this has caused me to feel insecure, hopeless, and useless at times.

Hang on, I am not speaking doom and gloom to you. The purpose of this letter is to allow God to gently apply SHEE-P-R to your heart. My prayer is that He will begin the compressions on your chest. Blood will start working its way through your spirit again.

Small Church ministry is tough mentally and statistically. Most pastors fall into a low-income bracket, which is tough when you are trying to raise a family. In Small Church Ministry you are essentially creating something out of nothing. When I was in Bible College, an esteemed professor made an impression on me when he would talk about the story of creation. The Latin word *Ex Nihilo* means "out of nothing." God created this world, the universe out of absolutely nothing. He is still creative in his process and has the power to create something out of nothing. We must trust in His abilities in our life. Pray that God would give you, or your family, your staff, your secretary, your team a large dose of "*Ex-Nihilo*" creativity.

Out of curiosity, what year did you gain your ministry credentials?

I was credentialed in 1990, and to this date I have never achieved the pinnacle of success in the world's eyes or for that matter, the church's eyes. I have never pastored a strong, vibrant, big budgeted, large membership, multiple ministry opportunity church. I have quit the ministry 869 times to this date. I have met some of the meanest, toughest, double-tongued people during my tenure of ministry, but I have been called to do this, and I am committed to that call.

The question again is… Why?

Ministry is hard.

To this date I have never been able to afford a new car, go on a cruise with my wife, have the latest in technology, be trendy in fashion, buy land or make enough money to make life more convenient. Sometimes I am tempted to ask the question, why do I do this? Why do I put up with these people? Why can't I afford to live a more padded life? Why do many of my friends seem to have an easier life than me?

This little story of mine is by no means a feel-sorry-for-me encroachment to my life… No, no, no… by all means, NO!

Why do I pastor?

Ministry is hard, but God is good!

That is why!

I will never forget the moment in my life when I knew that I was called to be in full time ministry. I was young, full of hopes and dreams. The life of a pastor seemed like a classy way to live-golf on Thursday, staff meeting on Tuesday, lunch with the mayor on Wednesday, preach on Sunday.

When you are young in the ministry the sky is bluer, the grass is greener, and you sing songs like "God is Great!" (Sampson 2001) and "How Great is our God" (Tomlin 2004). But sometimes when the reality of ministry hits you later in life you pull up the old country song, "Why me, Lord" (Kristofferson 1972)?

I have never regretted becoming a pastor. However, I have looked across the proverbial fence and noticed that other churches and ministries seemed to be more successful, powerful, and fun. I sometimes think to myself that the grass looks greener, plusher, and more beautiful over there. While on my side of the fence we seem to be facing a major drought and makes everything seem brown and burnt.

To my embarrassment, in my denomination most districts make available the "open church list" on their district websites. This is a directory of any open ministry position in that district from Lead Pastor to any form of assistants. I have caught myself shopping for a new church position like I am shopping for a new car. Is it close to water? Are there fun activities for my family to do? What is the cost of living? How big is the church?

Usually after some much-needed time on my knees, I have always concluded that God has placed me at my current location for a divine purpose, something bigger than myself. Jesus is my guide, my shepherd, my leader, and my friend. He has promised me over and over that He would never leave me or forsake me. He said that he would be closer than a brother.

A few years ago, I was told a story that goes something like this:

A young man was in the final days of a semester in college. His psychology professor made it clear that the final for the class was coming and everyone needed to be prepared for this comprehensive exam. The students spent hours preparing for this final. On the day of the final, the students were sitting in their rows of desks, #2 pencil was sharpened, and an alternative pencil was at the top of the desk. The professor made it clear that no one was to look at the test until he said "Go." The test laid upside down on each of the student's desks as the professor made that motion of "Go." To their surprise only one question was on the test... Why? You could feel the tension in the room rise as students hurried to make an impression on the professor with their clever and profound answers.

But this one student answered the question with two short words, turned in his test and was finished in less than two minutes. The professor awarded him with an "A" as he answered – Why not?

I am not sure if this story is a true story. But the moral of this story is one that everyone in ministry needs to consider. We say "Why?" as if we are living as martyrs, but we are not. We say "Why?" when our current ministry does not compare to a more successful ministry.

Your calling is to bring hope, peace, and light to the region that you were called to serve.

There is no doubt in my mind that you have heard the statement that the "Glass is half full" or the "Glass is half empty." I would like to remind you that your glass is half full. No question about it.

With God, you lack nothing.

Do not ask God, Why?

Ask yourself, Why not?

Faithfully Serving Jesus,

John McHaffie
Small Church Pastor

Dear Small Church Pastor,

*Y*ou must get excited about the amazing resources God has given to you.

Francis Schaeffer in his book "No Little People, No Little Places" writes, "As a Christian considers the possibility of being the Christian glorified, often his reaction is, 'I am so limited. Surely it does not matter much whether I am walking as a creature glorified or not.' Or, to put it another way, 'It is wonderful to be a Christian, but I am such a small person, so limited in talents—or energy or psychological strength or knowledge—that what I do is not really important'" (Schaeffer 2003).

The Bible, however, has quite a different emphasis: With God there are no little people.

Hebrews 11:32-34 -"And what shall I more say? for the time would fail me to tell of Gedeon, and of Barak, and of Samson, and of Jephthae; of David also, and Samuel, and of the prophets: Who through faith subdued kingdoms, wrought righteousness, obtained promises, stopped the mouths of lions. Quenched the violence of fire, escaped the edge of the sword, out of weakness were made strong, waxed valiant in fight, turned to flight the armies of the aliens" (King James Bible 2021).

These are the bible heroes the writer of Hebrews did not take the time to mention. Many of us fit quite securely into this group of the faithful, yet unrecognized. We may not be getting calls to preach at conventions and seminars, called to television interviews and being asked to pastor large churches. But God is using you where you are.

A basic understanding of living "Sent," or the role of an apostle is to bloom where you are planted. You must have a pioneer spirit in the spiritual realm and not stop until Jesus returns.

Keep aiming for the horizon!

For more information on the role of the apostle in today's church I highly recommend that you get a copy of <u>Apostolic Spark</u> by Jeff Hartensveld (Hartensveld 2014).

Faithfully Serving Jesus,

John McHaffie
Small Church Pastor

Dear Small Church Pastor,

Quitting is not an option!

Before you quit… Go to the library or online and check out Foxe's Book of Martyrs (Emerald House 2004) or Jesus Freaks (Baker Publishing 2014).

If you have read these books, you are better acquainted with persecution. I am not trying to compare my story with the stories in these great books on Christian Martyrdom, to say ministry is not hard and usually does not come with all the bells and whistles, we are ministers because it is simply a joy to know that we are being obedient to our Father.

We do not have the option to quit. We are in covenant with God. Sometimes, He calls us to places that do not seem to make sense, but we must trust his direction. Usually, we want to quit when we are discouraged and have been hurt or belittled by someone.

I am no stranger to quitting. On average, I quit about 869 times per year. I give up! I quit! I also look to see if the grass is greener on the other side.

A few years ago, a family friend was in a car accident and he died a few days later. A devastating blow to his church, friends, and his family. Susan, my wife, and I traveled four hours to be with this family and say our good-byes. On the way back home from the funeral we were having a heart-to-heart conversation about how unhappy we were and how the church people did not want to follow. You know the conversation. I am sure you have had many of them as well.

I told my wife I needed a sign, a real sign from God if we were to stick this assignment out. I was ready to begin to get rates from U-Haul, so we could move on.

Did you read the line earlier? Quitting is not an option! In my heart, I wanted to quit, but my spirit-man wanted to fight the good fight. We finally made it back home and before we went inside, we checked the mailbox to pick-up the mail. I received a letter from the IRS and told me that I had received the first-time homeowner's stimulus package. I needed to stay in my house for a total of three years, and if I break this agreement, I will owe the federal government that money plus interest. I said, "That is my sign!!!"

Since then, God really moved in some amazing ways in that church and in the community.

Never say die! Never quit!

Faithfull Serving Jesus,

John McHaffie
Small Church Pastor

Dear Small Church Pastor,

I was privileged to have a true gentleman in my church that really loved the Lord and longed to serve Him with all his heart. Al and I went out for pie and coffee about every other week and he just listened to me talk about ministry. What I loved about Al was his ability to be so positive about family, life, the ministry, and God. Al has been retired for several years and was locally known for his sayings, "We're family!" "It CAN be done!" "Teamwork makes the dream work!"

Al taught me to think positively and to serve with a passion that can only be found in knowing Christ. I understand that the more I learn the less I know about life. But I can always "trust in the Lord and lean not on my own understanding and in all your ways acknowledge Him and He will direct your path."

I remember as a kid, sitting through the altar call on a Sunday night service and it seemed without fail that the song by Bill and Gloria Gaither always ended up being sung during this prayer time. "I will serve thee because I love thee..." (Gaither 2011)

I will serve because I love!!!

It is not about me, but about HIM & THEM!!!

Romans 12:1-21 – "Therefore, I urge you, brothers and sisters, in view of God's mercy, to offer your bodies as a living sacrifice, holy and pleasing to God—this is your true and proper worship. Do not conform to the pattern of this world but be transformed by the renewing of your mind. Then you will be able to test and approve what God's will is—his good, pleasing, and perfect will. For by the grace given me I say to every one of you: Do not think of yourself more highly than you ought, but rather think of yourself with sober judgment, in accordance with the faith God has distributed to each of you. For just as each of us has one body with many members, and these members do not all have the same function, so in Christ we, though many, form one body, and each member belongs to all the others. We have different gifts, according to the grace given to each of us. If your gift is prophesying, then prophesy in accordance with your faith; if it is serving, then serve; if it is teaching, then teach; if it is to encourage, then give encouragement; if it is giving, then give generously; if it is to lead, do it diligently; if it is to show mercy, do it cheerfully. Love must be sincere. Hate what is evil; cling to what is good. Be devoted to one another in love. Honor one another above yourselves. Never be lacking in zeal, but keep your spiritual fervor, serving the Lord. Be joyful in hope, patient in affliction, faithful in prayer. Share with the Lord's people who are in need. Practice hospitality. Bless those who persecute you; bless and do not curse. Rejoice with those who rejoice; mourn with those who mourn. Live in harmony with one another. Do not be proud but be willing to associate with people of low position. Do not be conceited."

"Do not repay anyone evil for evil. Be careful to do what is right in the eyes of everyone. If it is possible, as far as it depends on you, live at peace with everyone. Do not take revenge, my dear friends, but leave room for God's wrath, for it is written: "It is mine to avenge; I will repay," says the Lord. On the contrary: "If your enemy is hungry, feed him; if he is thirsty, give him something to drink. In doing this, you will heap burning coals on his head. Do not be overcome by evil but overcome evil with good" (King James Bible 2021).

Did you find any possible ways to serve in this passage?

I know we get tired and worn out. I am not talking about burn-out, just being tired and worn out from serving, something that a couple days of respite will cure. Sometimes we get tired and worn out and this could lead to burnout, we can never give up, but always keep serving.

When I start feeling discouraged and want to give up, I watch the movie Facing the Giants. One of the most powerful scenes in that movie is the scene known at the "death crawl." The coach calls one of his players out and he tells him to come to him. He proceeds to blindfold him and puts another player on his back as he initiates the death crawl position.

Before the scene is over, this smart-mouthed-has-been is now realizing that he has much more within himself if he simply digs a little deeper.

That is true in most churches. We give up too soon. We become cynical and critical of our surrounding and have already accepted that we are on a losing team.

Romans says we all have different gifts. These gifts can be used to better serve our communities, churches, and each other.

A few years ago, I acquired "The Servant's Towel" as a gift given to the pastors and workers of a church in which I was on staff and I have kept this towel and the poem for years. This poem is very powerful and has been a great reminder for me that I must continue to serve.

The Servant's Towel

"...so, he got up from the meal, took off his outer clothing, and wrapped a towel around his waist." John 13:4

Do you own a Jesus towel, and do you always use it?

Have you thought about his piece of cloth and what made Jesus choose it?

Have you made your towel into a mantle and warmed a sister who is cold?

Did you wipe the sweat upon the brow of a brother with a load?

Will you make your towel a blanket to wrap a babe so sweet, or use your towel to cushion your neighbors blistered feet?

Will you make your towel a bandage for a sinner cut and bruised?

Will your towel protect the innocent from being beaten up and used?

Scrub a floor, dry a dish, wipe a tear or two, and use your towel in every way, like Jesus used to do.

Wear your towel from dawn to dawn and never leave it lie.

Make your towel a part of you until the day you die.

Worn and torn, it will become a robe of beauty bright.

Then enter in my faithful child, and rest in God's great light (Ross).

"...in as much as you have done it unto one of the least of these, you have done it unto me." Matthew 25:40 (King James Bible 2021).

Faithfully Serving Jesus,

John McHaffie
Small Church Pastor

Dear Small Church Pastor,

We have been called to love our neighbors. Here is another powerful equation to consider: Dirt + Divine = Supernatural

"Ministry takes place when divine resources meet human needs through loving channels to the glory of God." - Warren Wiersbe (Wiersebe 2007)

How can I love my neighbor? The answer to this question can be found in Leviticus 19:9-18:

Leviticus 19:9-10 – "And when ye reap the harvest of your land, thou shalt not wholly reap the corners of thy field, neither shalt thou gather the gleanings of thy harvest. And thou shalt not glean thy vineyard, neither shalt thou gather every grape of thy vineyard; thou shalt leave them for the poor and stranger: I am the Lord your God" (King James Bible 2021).

When you take a closer look at these verses you will notice that we should make provision for people who live in our neighborhoods that need sustenance. For some, this is a new way of thinking as we see in this verse that there is no command to give, but simply to provide food for those who are in need.

We should make integrity a practice in all our relationships. This verse says that you must eliminate lying, cheating, and stealing from the way you live. When there is a lack of integrity, usually you will find that there is a lack of treating others with love and compassion for the people in your neighborhood. Leviticus 19:11 - "'Do not steal. Do not lie. Do not deceive one another'" (King James Bible 2021).

Leviticus 19:12 – "And ye shall not swear by my name falsely, neither shalt thou profane the name of thy God: I am the Lord"

(King James Bible 2021). We must love our neighbor by understanding the nature of God and his purpose and love for mankind. Many times, we use God's name to get our way or a way that justifies harming someone else. There are more ways to take God's name in vain by using his name as a swear word, but when we use God's name it should be to speak life and not death into those who you meet each day.

Leviticus 19:13 – "Thou shalt not defraud thy neighbor, neither rob him: the wages of him that is hired shall not abide with thee all night until the morning" (King James Bible 2021). No one should ever grow rich by underpaying someone and claim that they love that person. We must treat our neighbors justly and fairly.

Leviticus 19:14 – "Thou shalt not curse the deaf, nor put a stumbling block before the blind, but shalt fear thy God: I am the Lord" (King James Bible 2021).

Compassion should be a value of every believer and church to lend a helping hand and to do whatever it takes to create an environment for anyone who has special needs. We should be going the extra mile to make everyone feel comfortable and to make our surroundings easy to navigate. Take a look at your restrooms, entry ways and classrooms to see if you have facilities that facilitate spiritual growth for those who have special needs.

Leviticus 19:15 – "Ye shall do no unrighteousness in judgment: thou shalt not respect the person of the poor, nor honor the person of the mighty: but in righteousness shalt thou judge thy neighbor" (King James Bible 2021). All people are to be viewed as having value! God sees us all as His children. In this passage, it says neither rich nor poor are to be chosen as honored. We are all created equal and all of us have certain rights and privileges that are not based on the ability to make money and contribute large sums of money.

You can love your neighbor by accepting them for who they are and not how much money they have made or have given to the church.

Leviticus 19:16 – "Thou shalt not go up and down as a tale-bearer among thy people: neither shalt thou stand against the blood of thy neighbor; I am the Lord" (King James Bible 2021). Use your words to speak the truth. Love is the truth. Love never needlessly brings harm to your neighbor. A believer should never be guilty of character assassination of anyone because everyone is your neighbor and the Bible clearly tells us to LOVE YOUR NEIGHBOR.

Leviticus 19:17 – "Thou shalt not hate thy brother in thine heart: thou shalt in any wise rebuke thy neighbor, and not suffer sin upon him" (King James Bible 2021). We should always reject any and all hateful thoughts. Hatred is the opposite of love and love is the direction that the Bible is pressing us to do. Thinking hateful thoughts is dangerous because it can result in hateful actions and can lead to poor decisions that you could regret for a lifetime.

This is a forgotten aspect of love. Love rebukes when it sees wrong. The purpose of this rebuke is to keep individuals from suffering from their sins. The one who is giving the rebuke must deliver it with complete love and the desire to have a redemptive conclusion to the situation.

Leviticus 19:18 – "Thou shalt not avenge, nor bear any grudge against the children of thy people, but thou shalt love thy neighbor as thyself: I am the Lord" (King James Bible 2021). As one who desires to love your neighbor, you should do everything in your power to not entertain wrong desires when it comes to dealing with grudges and thoughts of revenge. Love rules out every wrong desire for another's bad attitudes. When you rejoice in the misfortune of someone else, you violate the very act of love.

I will conclude with the words of Apostle Paul, "Love is patient, love is kind. It does not envy, it does not boast, it is not proud.

It does not dishonor others, it is not self-seeking, it is not easily angered, it keeps no record of wrongs. Love does not delight in evil but rejoices with the truth. It always protects, always trusts, always hopes, always perseveres. Love never fails. But where there are prophecies, they will cease; where there are tongues, they will be stilled; where there is knowledge, it will pass away" (King James Bible 2021).

Faithfully Serving Jesus,

John McHaffie
Small Church Pastor

Dear Small Church Pastor,

I am reminded of a historical site that has not withstood the test of time.

The Herodian Fortress was a massive fortress that King Herod built that overshadowed all of Bethlehem with a continued reminder of Herod's power and influence.

As you know, Herod was the king that was in power during the time of Christ birth, he was a powerful king and at the stroke of his pen he could create new laws with no discussion from any council. It was this king, at the time of Christ's birth, who sent forth an edict to have all baby boys under the age two slaughtered for he feared that a new king would come from that generation and overthrow his reign of power.

The Great Herodian was the third largest fortress in the world at the time that it was built. It was nearly the size of 45 footballs field, with swimming pools, and complete with all the luxuries that anyone could experience or imagine.

This was a massive fortress that was proclaiming Herod's greatness. But 2000 years later, it is a pile of rubble and has no significant value other than glancing at history or a place to visit on a Holy Land tour.

Pastor, you may have taken your current church, but you feel like you are in the shadow of the great Herodian. I am not meaning your predecessor is evil and longs to make your life miserable. But it seems every time you have a new idea you are continually reminded of the former days.

You have a decision to make concerning the Kingdom of God, you are called to be there for this present and immediate season.

So, lead!

It might take a few years to establish yourself, but my guess is, your predecessor did not make decisions simply to infuriate his future replacement. I am sure he prayed, sought God, fasted, much like you are doing. He invested his life in ministry, in community and in the church.

So, go be you!

Not him.

You were never meant to live in the shadow of any former pastors.

God chose you for this assignment. YOU! Not him, and not anyone else but you. Before the foundations of the world, he had a plan and purpose for you. God needs you right where you are.

Bloom where you are planted!

The interesting thing about the Great Herodian is that it still stands, not in the forefront, but in the background. Herod died and so did his massive kingdom. However, archaeologists have been extracting valuable history from there for many years. What if you start being an archaeologist at your current location and begin to dive in carefully uncovering the past victories, past hurts, past drama, building plans, failed plans, successful outreaches and begin to dream about the possibilities you have to reach a new group of people that God has called you to.

Stop looking at the Great Herodian with fear and trepidation and grab a shovel, a sifter and start digging and dreaming about tomorrow.

Faithfully serving Jesus

John McHaffie
Small Church Pastor

SECTION THREE

Pain & Self-Care

"*God never wastes an ounce of pain.*" -Mary Palmer

Dear Small Church Pastor,

$\mathcal{I}$ want to give you a little insight on my personality type and why I am the way I am.

I am an INFJ personality type via the Myers/Briggs Type Indicator (Briggs 1987).

What does this mean?

The INFJ personality leans toward Introversion, Intuiting, Feeling and Judging.

- Introversion (I): INFJs tend to be reserved, quiet and have à small circle of close friends.
- Intuition (N): INFJs prefer abstract concepts and tend to focus on the big picture rather than concrete details.
- Feeling (F): INFJs place a greater emphasis on personal concerns than objective facts when making decisions.
- Judging (J): INFJs like to exert control by planning, organizing, and making decisions as early as possible.

People with INFJ personalities tend to exhibit the following characteristics:

- Idealistic
- Sensitive to the needs of others
- Highly creative and artistic
- Reserved
- Focused on the future.
- Private
- Values close, deep relationships
- Enjoys thinking about the meaning of life.

Why do I feel the need to need to give you my personality assessment information?

My purpose in this writing you this letter is to encourage you, because you are called to Rural America or small churches to encourage the local church leadership and pastors who feel inadequate in their daily church functions.

My intention is simple and pure. I have compassion and empathy for the heartbroken, confused, and isolated pastors in the small towns and small churches across this nation.

I wanted you to hear a fellow small church pastor that is not a well-known leader of a multi-site campus, mega church or even our mini-mega churches. I am a classic introvert with a normal call of God on my life and want to develop the conversation to encourage you to continue loving the people that God assigned to you.

I hope you find the encouragement in these few words to love your church and community as you serve the mayor, business owner, farmer, rancher, truck driver, teacher, police officer, firemen, lawyer, judge, doctor in the town you serve.

Faithfully Serving Jesus,

John McHaffie
Small Church Pastor

Dear Small Church Pastor,

I love to read from great godly leaders that have learned humility from their triumphs and their tragedies. Tommy Barnett says, "There is a miracle in your house" (Barnett 1996).

Everything you need to accomplish the next phase of your church life is already present and accounted for. You do not need to look any further than what you already have. You have miracles all around you, resources at your fingertips.

Several years ago, the worship leader at the church I pastored, felt it was time to step down and move on from her current role as music minister. I took a deep breath because I knew that I was now the new worship leader. For several weeks, I led worship in a sanctuary with my guitar, a bassist and one other background singer in a sanctuary that could seat 400 plus, but our attendance was 45 at the most.

The 45 souls in attendance were scattered throughout that auditorium and it was difficult to hear the singing of the congregation. About 4 weeks into my new position of worship leader, I recruited my 10-year-old son to thump the bass drum in hopes of getting a little more dynamic out of our worship service. My 12-year-old son reminded me that I had taught him some power chords and he too wanted in on the action.

Now, I have my guitar, a bass, singer, and 10-year-old who cannot see over the set of drums and a 12-year-old who has played a total of two weeks. Let's worship!

Several months into this temporary set up of worship mayhem, I began to complain to God. "Why can't we have a NORMAL worship team that sings NORMAL worship songs? Why, why, why?" I remember that day so clearly. The Lord spoke to my heart and said to me, "If I answer your prayer, then these boys will not be able to play anymore, and I have great plans for them." I bowed my head, repented and I can proudly say that my kids are leading worship every week to this day and the spirit of God is all over them. I had a miracle in my house, they were just very young and would require my time and attention to develop their ministry gifts.

The exciting part of this story, at this writing, my oldest son is on staff at a great church and leads worship anytime he gets a chance while my other son is finishing up his pre-med studies and will play drums on a worship team anytime he is asked.

Faithfully Serving Jesus,

John McHaffie
Small Church Pastor

Dear Small Church Pastor,

Pain - Oh, how I hate this subject!
I need to continue a story I started in an earlier letter about a group of people who left the church.

The next day, one day after they left, I was sitting in a district leadership forum. Let me tell you, I was broken! Oh, the pain! The agony! How could those people not like me, or trust my ministry style?

Half-way through the morning session the speaker stops and says, "I really have a burden for a couple of pastors in our meeting that need prayer."

"Oh no," I thought, "This is not me." As he kept talking, I began to cry like a baby in front of everyone! The speaker asked me and another gentleman to come forward, because he wanted to lay hands on and pray over us for direction and peace.

The speaker gave this beautiful word of knowledge to this other minister who was obviously going through a tough time, and then he asked me to pray for the other guy.

I was offended! I was hurting! I was having a hard time praying because I had been hurt the day before by people who I thought were my friends and colleagues.

So, I reluctantly prayed for him. I will never forget this moment. It was like a lightning bolt went through my body and I prayed for this man with power that I had never felt before.

The speaker then gently asked us to sit down. Prayer time was over. I was offended again! I needed a Word from God. I felt like I had been ripped off and I deserved that Word. After all, I was feeling a bit of pain from the recent attacks against my character. I felt like I knew what the Word was going to be... something like

75

this… "John, my worthy servant, you have been hurt by perilous people, and I the Lord your God, the God of Abraham, Isaac, and Jacob will infest the armpits of those who have hurt you with the fleas of a thousand camels."

The speaker asked us to sit down and then he had the nerve to simply finish his lesson that he had started a couple of hours ago. Then, he dismissed us for lunch, and I wanted to scream. "Where's my special Word from the Lord?"

I submitted to my leadership and reluctantly went to lunch and came back for session two.

Fifteen minutes before session two was finished, the speaker stopped and starred at me. He said, "John, I have a word for you, but I don't understand it and I want to give it to you in front of these witnesses." I froze… yes, it is time. Here it comes, a devastating word to all those people who had revolted against God's anointed.

The speaker reluctantly said, "John, the Lord is getting ready to increase your capacity for pain."

"What?" "Wait, what about the camels, fleas, armpits… Your anointed… God… What?" "NO! I want revenge!"

This was not the Word that I wanted to hear. I wanted revenge, but God wanted my undivided attention.

I hate pain!

God was getting ready to increase my pain threshold and I was not overly excited about this moment.

I have since adopted a quote from my mother-in-law, "God never wastes an ounce of pain!"

I did not want more pain. The pain that I had felt days earlier was enough for me. I did not want to learn anymore in the school of pain. I wanted only one thing, and that was to graduate with my degree and move on.

I will speak more to this pain in a future letter. Until then, get ready for God to use every part of you, even your most painful experiences.

Faithfully Serving Jesus,

John McHaffie
Small Church Pastor

Dear Small Church Pastor,

*I*n my most recent letter to you, I shared with you how a group of people left my church one Sunday morning and it broke my heart. The next day, a special word of knowledge was given to me, "God was going to increase my capacity for pain."

Three months later, I was standing in the office of an oncologist at the Children's Hospital.

Processing what was happening in my family. My blue-eyed, blond haired four-year-old daughter was diagnosed with cancer, a rare form of melanoma and I was beginning to feel a pain level increase in my life.

Confused. Hurt. Devastated.

I would rarely make it from the doctor's office to my minivan in the parking garage without breaking down in deep, painful, outburst of tears and sincere sobs. This pain stung deeply into my soul and that pain never left my conscious mind, it was a twenty-four-seven reminder.

The oncologist, at one point, said that Emily needed surgery as soon as possible, because the cancer had made it to her lymph system. I asked if we could have some time to pray and think about it. He used the word "fatal" in his preliminary diagnosis. We needed to have her in surgery within a week from the official diagnosis and biopsy.

You want to talk about pain!

This was pain… Pain like I have never experienced.

My little girl had 3 surgeries before her 5th birthday and her cancer treatments continued for over a year.

There was a point during this situation I reevaluated my own personal pain threshold. The pain level I had experienced from the agitated church folk months ago did not compare to the pain that I had experienced with my daughter's bout with cancer.

[**For the record:** Emily is cancer free, and she was a beast on the varsity volleyball team for all four years of High School]

I have never looked at pain the same.

I rarely allow church problems and situations to get me down and out. God has used this pain for his glory, and I am telling you firsthand. God cannot fully use you until you are broken and spilled out.

If you are experiencing pain, just wait, He is not far away. Remember, you can always cast your cares and burden on Jesus, for He care for you.

Faithfully Serving Jesus,

John McHaffie
Small Church Pastor

Dear Small Church Pastor,

*S*erving is the vehicle that is fueled by compassion. We were all called to serve.

Have you ever heard anyone make the comment, "It's not my calling," or "That is not my spiritual gift?"

When circumstances arise in our lives, and we are not in our comfort zone, we typically default our own thinking to become passive about serving. Jesus made no bones about it. He came to serve.

A few years ago, when I arrived in Milwaukee to my first senior pastorate, I was introduced to a little machine that I had never used before, or ever want to use again, at least that is what I thought. It was the Tim-the-Toolman Snowblower 2000. Anyway, it was a beast of a machine that got the job done, and I got to know this machine extremely well the first couple of years in Milwaukee.

Our church and parsonage sat right on the corner of two major streets. The church property was a three-acre lot, which meant we had twice the number of sidewalks to keep clear of ice and snow and that brownish-gray substance the snowplows would leave behind.

Little did I know at the time, it snowed one-hundred inches per winter. Wow, that was a lot of snow blowing. Every morning I had to get up and make sure the sidewalks were clear before the daycare staff arrived and before the city cited us with a ticket for code violation for failing to clear sidewalks.

It just so happened on one very cold, Milwaukee morning and I was not in a good mood. I was already grumbling before the coffee pot had finished perking its life giving, hot-caffeine jolt. I stormed out of the parsonage, opened the garage door, and began a familiar cadence of my morning task.

I was halfway finished with this process of walking behind this beast of a machine and suddenly a chunk of ice breaks free from the frozen sidewalk and is sucked up into this massive snow blower, destroying the snow shoot. Then, it turned ever-so-perfectly and throws the remaining snow into my face.

I had enough.

I shoved that snow blower into a snowbank and like a raging lunatic, I began to tell God what I thought of His snow blower and His horrible weather. I yelled at God at the intersection of Layton Avenue and 116th Street that morning and said, "God, I think there is a better way to use my college degree than this!" I began to push the snow blower back to the garage where it belonged. When I got to the garage, I lifted the door with a thrust of anger and shoved the snow blower as hard as I could and then slammed the door and went back inside of my parsonage.

My wife saw my snow-covered body and I said to her, "I don't want to hear any of your thoughts on how beautiful you think snow is, I hate this stuff!" Then I proceeded to get my hot shower to prepare for my day.

I was in my office that afternoon, and I felt the need to go spend some time at the altar. I felt the Lord speaking to me saying, "I know a great way to spend your college degree, serve me!" It was crystal clear, I turned to the story in John 13, where Jesus did not long for a title, but He grabbed a towel and began to serve.

I am not proud of my attitude on that day, but I am happy that it was a teachable moment that allowed God to help me work through some of my selfish theology and realign my heart to serve him.

This might be a great time to grab your Bible and turn to John 13, reread this familiar passage, and look intently at the word serve and then begin to pray and ask God how you can serve Him more effectively.

Faithfully Serving Christ,

John McHaffie
Small Church Pastor

Dear Small Church Pastor,

*C*ompassion is to feel the pain of another so deeply that we are compelled to do something about it. People in Bible times believed that the seat of emotions was found in the intestinal area. That is why the King James Version uses the phrase, "bowels of mercy."

"To get inside someone's skin until we can see things with his eyes, think things with his mind, and feel things with his feelings; to move in and act on behalf of those who are hurting." -William Barclay (Barclay 2016, 3).

Matthew 14:14 - And Jesus went forth, and saw a great multitude, and was moved with compassion toward them, and he healed their sick.

The word "compassion" literally means that Jesus was so moved that His stomach churned, or literally, "his bowels yearned" for the crowd. He saw the need and then He went into action.

Compassion must move us to action.

Compassion is a characteristic of God that the Bible reveals this part of His divine nature:

> Deuteronomy 4:31 - "For the LORD your God is a merciful God…" (King James Bible 2021).

> Nehemiah 9:31 – "Nevertheless for thy great mercies' sake thou didst not utterly consume them, nor forsake them; for thou art a gracious and merciful God" (King James Bible 2021).

Psalm 119:132 – "Look thou upon me, and be merciful unto me, as thou usest to do unto those that love thy name" (King James Bible 2021).

Daniel 9:18 - "O my God, incline thine ear, and hear; open thine eyes, and behold our desolations, and the city which is called by thy name: for we do not present our supplications before thee for our righteousnesses, but for thy great mercies" (King James Bible 2021).

Micah 7:18-19 – "Who is a God like unto thee, that pardoneth iniquity, and passeth by the transgression of the remnant of his heritage? he retaineth not his anger forever, because he delighteth in mercy. He will turn again, he will have compassion upon us; he will subdue our iniquities; and thou wilt cast all their sins into the depths of the sea" (King James Bible 2021).

Romans 9:16 - "It does not, therefore, depend on man's desire or effort, but on God's mercy" (King James Bible 2021).

Ephesians 2:4 - "...God, who is rich in mercy" (King James Bible 2021).

James 5:11- "The Lord is full of compassion and mercy" (King James Bible 2021).

Compassion gives food to the hungry, comforts the grieving, gives love to the rejected, forgiveness to the offender, and companionship to the lonely. Jesus certainly demonstrated compassion and He expected His followers to show compassion as well. It is in our nature to criticize, be bitter and withhold forgiveness. It is also way too natural for us to ignore real needs of our community when we witness them, because we are wrapped up in our to-do list. You should love your community with the same compassion Jesus had on the crowds.

Faithfully Serving Christ,

John McHaffie
Small Church Pastor

Dear Small Church Pastor,

$\mathscr{S}$everal years ago, I came across an amazingly beautiful book that was written in 1652 called "A Priest to the Temple or, The Country Parson His CHARACTER, and Rule of Holy Life." The Author, Mt. G. H. (Pick a File 2021)

In this book, the author addresses the importance of the Country Parson to be faithful to the call of God and be obedient to the cause of Christ in the community to which he would be entrusted. The concept of the Parson was to be the *Cura Animarum* or the *Cure of Souls*. In essence this, position was to be the priest or the Doctor of souls for that community with the understanding that "I shall not harm."

"The exercise of a clerical office involving the instruction by sermons, admonitions and the sanctification through the sacraments of the faithful in a determined district by a person legitimately appointed for the purpose." -Catholic Encyclopedia (Catholic Answers 2021)

I know this is not where we generally find our position papers on Kingdom Authority and apostleship, but for a moment could I challenge you about your calling from this old writing. These men who were to be the *Cura Animarum* of that position and they had given themselves to celibacy and vowed to be the Parson who could be trusted throughout life's many ebbs and flows.

Can you imagine pastoring without your cell phone, laptop, tablet, housing allowance, company car, benefits package, and expense account?

My purpose in introducing you to this incredibly old book is for you to recognize these men gave up everything to move to a region that was foreign to them and to bring a hope of Christ in everyday community life. The role of the rural pastor has everything to do with the care, the nourishment and spiritual well-being, the protection and oversight of souls, to see that Christ is their Prophet, Priest and King.

In 1652, I am to believe that the Catholic church gave this manual to each of their parsons with the intent that each of them would be favored by the community and community leaders to lead, guide and direct them in spiritual paths.

Here is the index of topics that were recorded for all parsons to live by:

1. Of a Pastor.
2. Their Diversities
3. The Parson's Life
4. The Parson's Knowledge
5. The Parson's Accessary Knowledge
6. The Parson's Praying
7. The Parson's Preaching
8. The Parson on Sunday's
9. The Parson's State of Life
10. The Parson in his house
11. The Parson's Courtesies.
12. The Parson's Charity.
13. The Parson's Church.
14. The Parson in a Circuit.
15. The Parson Comforting.
16. The Parson a Father.
17. The Parson in Journey.
18. The Parson in Sentinel.
19. The Parson in reference.
20. The Parson in God's Stead.

21. The Parson Catechizing.
22. The Parson n Sacraments.
23. The Parson's Completeness.
24. The Parson Arguing.
25. The Parson Punishing.
26. The Parson's eye.
27. The Parson in mirth.
28. The Parson in Contempt.
29. The Parson with his Churchwardens.
30. The Parson's Consideration of Providence.
31. The Parson in Liberty.
32. The Parson's Surveys.
33. The Parson's Library.
34. The Parson's Dexterity in applying of Remedies.
35. The Parson's Condescending.
36. The Parson Blessing.
37. Concerning Detraction.
38. The Author's Prayer before Sermon.
39. A Prayer after Sermon.

I pray that you are the Cure of Souls where God has planted you. I pray that you run hard to the horizon. I pray that "Never give in, never give in, never, never, never, never—in nothing, great or small, large or petty—never give in except to convictions of honor and good sense" (Israel 2013).

Faithfully Serving Jesus,

John McHaffie
Small Church Pastor

SECTION FOUR

Obedience

Yielding to God even if you do not feel like it.

Dear Small Church Pastor,

I often think about the church and its condition, even when I am not "on-duty."
You know you are a rural pastor when...

- Most of the congregation has the same last name.
- When there are more actors in the Christmas play than people to watch it.
- One phone call fulfills your share of the prayer chain call list.
- You are expected to be at every function.
- You take up an extra offering to purchase toilet tissue for the bathrooms.

When I ponder feelings about the church in rural America, I cannot help but hear the voice of comedian Jeff Foxworthy telling me "redneck" jokes. "You Might Be a Redneck if..."

1. The Salvation Army declines your mattress.
2. You cut your grass and found a car.
3. You own a home that is mobile and 5 cars that are not.
4. You think the stock market has a fence around it.
5. Your stereo speakers used to belong to the Drive-in Theater.
6. Your boat has not left the driveway in 15 years.
7. You own a homemade fur coat.
8. Chiggers are included on your list of top 5 hygiene concerns.
9. You burn your yard rather than mow it.
10. If your wife has ever said, "Come move this transmission so I can take a bath."

Thank you, Jeff Foxworthy (Brainy Quotes 2021).

As we laugh at some of these "redneck" jokes and with a nod of the head we admit some of these might hit "closer" to home than others, one must take an honest assessment of rural America in relationship to the Great Commission and the Great Commandment.

We live in a society that loves meeting at Starbucks, the use of smart phones, or anything that helps us climb the ladder of success quickly and easily. Jesus makes himself clear when he said, "Go into all the world and preach the gospel to every creature." This well-known verse is recognized as a command not a suggestion! "all-of-the-world" and to "every-creature."

Rural America is often looked upon as a good steppingstone for future ministry than a current mission field all to itself. Most of us have been led to believe that we deserve a good salary with great benefits and develop a large staff, team leadership to assist us in our ministry. Rural ministry should be a destination, not a steppingstone.

Seldom do we hear pastors praying, "I will go where you want me to go, Lord." Many times, we find ourselves longing for a good cup of expensive coffee more than a desire to serve Jesus with unselfish abandonment and obedience in a faraway place without anyone knowing we even exist and without the convenience of a large stores, malls, and theaters.

A few years ago, I had the privilege of leading several missions' trips to the country of Cambodia. Cambodia is a nation that has experienced genocide by Pol Pot and the national government beyond our comprehension. I visited the museum where many innocent lives were cut short by this raving madman. Many Cambodians were laid to rest by the masses in a place known as the *Killing Fields*. I will never forget the images and the blood stains on the concrete walls and floors of that prison and torture chambers.

Three decades have passed and this country is now starting to recover from that awful remembrance of recent history. To this day, most people in Cambodia live in extreme poverty, yet they are extremely grateful for their freedom despite their horrific past.

While ministering in several small Cambodian villages, I looked at their dirty faces, played games, ate strange food, looked into their deep brown eyes, and a glowing smile on their little faces. Even though we were alien strangers we were greeted with a traditional Asian bow coupled with lots of love and kindness.

Our vans would roll into these small little villages loaded down with rice, oil, spices, water, and medications. People would line up for hours just to get a couple of Rolaids and Tylenol to aid them in temporary relief of their medical condition. Most of the medical problems that we faced were beyond our abilities and facilities, but we had the capability to administer prayer, love, and kindness with a whole lot of joy.

I had one of those "God" moments one day when I was minding my own business, saturated in my own pride, and joyfully thinking about all the good that I had done while I was ministering in Cambodia. The Lord spoke to my heart and shared with me a truth that changed my direction. I realized that we too had a similar need in America. Our rural communities need people who are called by God to "go to the ends of the earth," and share his love, hope, and compassion.

"To the ends of the earth," has a special ring to it. "To the ends of the earth," sounds so adventurous, mysterious, and even biblical. "To the ends of the earth," means relocation to a land that requires immunizations and language school. But "To the ends of the earth," might be 15 miles from where you are sitting right now. "To the ends of the earth," is everywhere! "To the ends of the earth," is NOWHERE.

Rural America can seem unattractive to someone seeking adventure, because of its reputation of being boring, predictable, and appearing to lack any type of adventure. However, when it is God's idea, you may be in for the ride of your life if you trust Him with all your heart, soul, mind, and strength.

Faithfully Serving Jesus,

John McHaffie
Small Church Pastor

Dear Small Church Pastor,

*I*f you are like me, you love when a missionary comes to your church and gives a fiery presentation of the gospel, as well as stories to make everyone weep with compassion.

Missionary stories are the best!

A few years ago, I was listening to a missionary speak about his lifetime of ministry. I regret the fact that I do not remember his name or what country he was ministering in, but his story left a life-changing effect on me. He was extremely frustrated at how non-productive he had been for the kingdom of God.

During one of his moments of self-pity, the Lord spoke to his heart and said, "Walk your neighborhoods and this community and pray for these dear people." And so, he did. He faithfully walked the neighborhood and community and he called on God to reach these people with the gospel of God's grace. As he walked and prayed, he would do his best to articulate their names, and/or house numbers to God. He would pray for healings, kids, purpose, and whatever else the Lord laid on his heart on that day.

A few months later in his personal prayer time, he had been faithful to pray for the individual homes, families, and other needs, the Lord spoke to his heart and said, "No one has ever mentioned their name to me!" "Thank-you!"

I froze in my chair and had one of those moments of a divine epiphany where my life was forever branded by that moment with a simple passion to pray for the people that might not have ever been prayed for. Since that time, I find myself walking and praying for people that I might never meet, interceding for people who would never invite me in their homes, but people who need to hear the greatest message that could forever change their life.

Rural America, for the most part, feels extremely spiritual, but is highly unreached and religiously superficial. Rural America seems to have a trace of Christianity, but the love of Jesus has never been practiced or penetrated the lives of most people. So, what can you do? Walk & pray! (Just as a side note, I would carry a big stick when you walk and pray – just in case you run into a snake or a big dog)

My challenge to you is to visualize rural America as a land of opportunity for a great harvest, not a steppingstone, or a place to pastor before you retire. Plant yourself. Give. Love. Be available for these small American villages that need less religion and more demonstration of the characteristics of Jesus.

Faithfully Serving Jesus,

John McHaffie
Small Church Pastor

Dear Small Church Pastor,

$\mathcal{H}$ere are staggering statistics concerning rural America found in the Convoy of Hope-Rural Compassion Training Handbook. I thought you would be interested in these numbers, for you and I share the same love for rural people.

- There are approximately 250 consistently poor counties in the United States; 244 of those are rural. The child poverty rates in these jurisdictions often exceed 35 percent.
- One of six children (2.5 million) living in rural regions of the United States are trapped in deep poverty, suffering from poor education and health.
- Rural children are 50 percent more likely than their urban peers to lack health insurance.
- A rural 8th grade student is 105 percent more likely more to have taken amphetamines; 75 percent more likely to have consumed cocaine, and 38% more likely to have smoked marijuana than his/her urban peers.
- The rural working poor are more likely to be economically insolvent and yet unsupported by welfare than their urban counterparts.
- Two-thirds of the rural poor have one family member that works.
- 57 percent of the rural poor do not have reliable transportation.

After reading these statistics I find myself dreaming about ways to offset these negative patterns of this world. In Romans 12:2, Paul says not to conform to the pattern of this world but be transformed by the renewing of your mind. As pastors, we can help people stuck in poverty, drugs, etc. by helping them to change their patterns and lifestyles and allowing Jesus to renew their minds to gain new hope and purpose.

I feel like I can do something. Feed a child, open a pantry in the school, start a tutoring program at the church or the school, offer activities that keep people from being bored or reverting to old habits.

We need to create environments that help change patterns from the world to the Word. If we do this, we will change America.

Faithfully Serving Jesus,

John McHaffie
Small Church Pastor

Dear Small Church Pastor,

I landed home from my third short term missions' trip to Cambodia, I began to research the growing needs in our rural communities. This new "God-moment" hit me like a sledge-hammer right in the heart. I began to ask tough questions concerning rural America...

- Why is it easier to take water, oil, and rice to a poor village in Cambodia, yet forsake the growing need in the interior of America's heartland?
- Does our church and denomination prepare men and women for the Rural Mission field?
- What strategy must we adopt to reach these who live in the not-so-far-away-rural places in rural America?

What was I going to do about this new burden?

I responded quickly with my Mosaic eloquence, "What if they do not believe me or listen to me?" Exodus 4:13, "O Lord, please send someone else to do it" (King James Bible 2021). I explained to the Lord that I was not a good candidate to begin to minister in rural America because I loved Starbucks way too much. "God, I have a problem with this! I do not hunt, and I don't enjoy hunting! God, I don't even like to fish" (King James Bible 2021)! A matter of fact, I do not really like to eat fish (no offense to Jesus who fed fish to 5000 people). "God, I don't own a truck! Why are you doing this to me?"

As I felt this new rural ministry mantle on my life, my response was very immature, because I did not get it.

I felt my time in my current church had come to an end. I began to research the new possibilities of my newfangled marching orders, I sent my resume' to several larger cities, larger churches in more affluent areas of the mid-west, all of which were located within a 1-mile radius of Starbucks.

It never crossed my mind that I was to be a pastor in a small, remote rural community in Southwest Missouri. Little did I know, the place that God was sending me did not have a Wal-Mart, movie theater, bowling alley, professional sports and one of the toughest things I read on the demographic report, NO STARBUCKS. Fortunately, God had put in place a better-than-Starbucks-experience in this small rural community– A hometown coffee roaster called Keen Bean Coffee Roasters. Yum!

I humbly dealt with my own frustrations of where God was leading me, as he led me on a Bible study of the life and ministry of the apostle Paul. The apostle Paul and I have nothing in common, other than our faith in Jesus.

Paul was a very tenacious-type-A personality. He was a strong leader, matter of fact, incredibly detailed and when he commanded his request, it-got-done. I, on the other hand, am not a type-A leader, I am more of the traditional, birth-order-middle-child personality. I would not call myself a people pleaser, but I seem to care what others think and tend to ask for more input in a situation than most people with a type A personality might tolerate.

While studying Apostle Paul, I realized I was a whole lot more like Barnabas, the encourager! Not, the bigger-than-life missionary who carries the message of the gospel on his shoulders around the world. I am usually the one that takes the "John Marks" of life and helps them overcome their moments of failure. So, why would God lead me to Apostle Paul's life for a personal confirmation?

The apostle Paul was a man who understood leadership and the need for people to change to this new paradigm of God's plan. Change is always essential for a new strategy.

Let us take a bird's eye view of this story.

We see Saul's actions early in the book of Acts serving up a platter of hatred to this new group of people known as "The Way." It was in his training, his purpose, his calling to eradicate this new form of false religion that was taking Jerusalem by storm.

As Saul and his company were traveling on their next business trip, something happened. I am not sure exactly what it was, but the Bible says that he was struck down by a great light and Jesus asked him a simple question. "Why are you persecuting me?" In this moment, everything changed. His purpose, his calling, his passion, and his life!

In this story, we see the beginning of a new creation in Christ. He now was donning a new passion, a new calling and in this incident, he was given a new name.

The power of Jesus changes the very core of our value system, the very foundation on which we have based our existence. The apostle Paul was changed in an instant! Over the next decade, Paul would receive training and inspiration as God was developing him to be a great apostle that would take the gospel of God's grace to the world.

This is an amazing story, but there is a greater reason for me to take a deeper look at Apostle Paul, but this would not happen until Acts 16. The beginning of Acts is pivotal and passionate for me and my calling. We see the power of God poured out in a physical demonstration to all who were present. We read about Peter preaching and 3,000 people received the message of the gospel of God's grace and the church began to grow exponentially.

The audience of this new church plant in the first seven chapters of Acts is the story of the Hebrew believers that are being transformed from only the law of Moses to the gospel of God's grace the by the acceptance of Jesus Christ as Messiah.

By the time we get to Acts chapter 10, we are not seeing as much of Apostle Peter, and we are hearing much more about Apostle Paul and the plans on taking this message to the Gentiles "to the ends of the earth" (King James Bible 2021).

The apostle Paul, with his companions, is beginning to move into missionary mode and the world would never be the same.

In Acts 16, Paul has a dream. This is no ordinary dream. In this dream, Paul sees a man that looks like, has attributes of and seems to be from the region of Macedonia.

Change, again?

Stop and wait a minute.

So, what?

I have had plenty of dreams and they have not made me change my direction or course in my life. My dreams are not usually the kind of dreams that I want to repeat, because of the weirdness, and peculiarity of them. However, I have a recurring dream of being back in college, behind in my assignments and failing a class, but, I usually wake up and realize this is a dream and go back to sleep realizing I have a college degree and usually within minutes I am back to dreamland.

Paul's dream is much different than my dreams. He sees a specific guy. He recognizes this man is from Macedonia. Was it his accent, clothing, color of skin? I am not sure, but this is a significant change for Paul. Instead of his travel plans leading him into the Orient, he is now making his travel arrangements to Europe.

Have you ever had a Macedonian call?

Have you ever been doing ministry with the right heart, attitude and obedience and the Lord gives you a sign, burden, or a desire to "go to the ends of the earth?" You know something is about to change, but you are not sure what it will be. You have a desire to go to another country, the inner city, or as in my case, rural America.

My calling to rural America did not come in the form of dream or even an initial desire. It was clear to my wife and me, through some confirmations that our newest level of obedience would be in a small unknown place and with little resources.

Throughout the years, God has placed righteous people to invest in the call of ministry that God was developing in me. A piece of advice that was given to me as a young man, and this advice has never left my side, is "You are not called to youth ministry, you are not called to children's ministry, you are called to obedience."

Paul was obedient! A few chapters earlier Paul was struck down with a great light and spiritual change happened. In Acts 16 he experiences change, yet again. His plans were not necessarily God's plans. They were not bad plans, but they were just not God's plan. So, the Apostle Paul responded and obeyed what the Lord had placed in his heart and dream.

Many of us get really good ideas. Not necessarily God ideas, but good ideas. We struggle day-to-day in ministry and wonder why God is not blessing our efforts. Possibly God has been speaking to you, but you are so inclined to see your dreams fulfilled and have failed to ask God's blessing over your hard work.

Have you had a Macedonian call?

Change of plan?

You are heading east, and God is saying, "Go west young man" (Smith 1990).

I really believe in my heart that God has been trying to get the attention of good, godly people to invade the darkness of rural

America. Forget about accomplishments. Forget about status or what your college friends will think about you going to some ghost town without a Starbucks.

Are you willing to listen? Or does that thought scare you out of your Justin Boots?

Faithfully Serving Jesus,

John McHaffie
Small Church Pastor

Dear Small Church Pastor,

When I felt like the Holy Spirit was prompting me to write these letters, I was busy developing an argument with God concerning my lack of writing skills, intelligence, and lack of effective leadership skills. I am a simple man, with hopes of hearing Jesus say, "Well done, thou good and faithful servant." But that is all. I do not feel like I have the personality, authority, or ability to speak into your life.

In his book, "The Circle Maker," Mark Batterson shared the story how he was a frustrated writer for 13 years and began to pray circles around his dream to write. As many of you know, Mark is a fantastic writer, pastor, speaker, and leader in the church today. He shares in his book, "I didn't write that book, I prayed that book" (Batterson 2016).

That one powerful sentence pierced my heart! God was saying to me, "Barnabas" I want to use you to encourage a group of people that need to hear your story about obedience. So, this is a simple prayer, written by a simple man to encourage you to stay strong and serve the quaint communities across our great country.

My story is more than likely not any different than your story. I do not have the experience of pastoring a huge church, I have never had millions of dollars run through my fingertips and I have not been asked to be a guest host on TBN. As a matter of fact, I almost did not write these letters because I felt inadequate and unqualified to share my pastoral story, to me, my life and ministry lacks pizzazz and I fear my story is not necessary, interesting, or important.

Not everyone is going to be as robust as Apostle Paul, Apostle Peter, or Apostle John, but as I read the book of Acts and other stories in the Bible, my eyes are drawn to the heroes who did not have a big name but had a huge role in the life of the church.

We all have the ability to be like Barnabas, the encourager. There is nothing wrong with being the one who helps restore people back into the Kingdom of God one life at a time, one cup of coffee at a time, one Bible study at a time.

Keep loving, keep encouraging, and keep on keeping on for the glory of God.

Faithfully Serving Jesus,

John McHaffie
Small Church Pastor

Dear Small Church Pastor,

I remember an experience my wife and I had as we were leaving the hustle and bustle of lower Manhattan from a fun-filled day in New York City. The noise of the city began to get quieter as our ferry boat departed from lower Manhattan and headed slowly for the docks of Staten Island. As we were about half-way across New York harbor, I stared at the enormous towers and all the other beautifully lit buildings as the light from their windows somehow seemed to be staring at me. In God's simple, but sure way, he spoke to my heart and said, "All of those windows represent someone's story." At that very instant, I had that "ah-ha moment" that took me to the Psalms where it says, "You are fearfully and wonderfully made" (King James Bible 2021). God intends for each of us to tell our story, not to bury it or place it on a shelf. He intends to use our story to make His name great. The book of Revelation clearly states that "we are over-comers by the Blood of the Lamb, and the Word of our Testimony."

God wanted me to share my story. For most of you, this is your story. Your story is a lot like mine and perceived as no story at all! God is wanting for you to tell your story of how His story speaks that Jesus is the hope and salvation of the world.

The church that I was sent to pastor was in a small southwest Missouri community with the population a little over four-thousand inhabitants, this community had no Wal-Mart, no big-name chain restaurants, except your basic fare of Taco Bell, McDonald's, Subway, and KFC.

This was quite a transition from my former assignment, which was in a major city within three miles radius I had access to four Starbucks, four shopping malls, Wal-Mart Super-Center, MLB, big-city ambiance, beautiful downtown, NBA, a great lake, tons of golf, and a ridiculously cool park district.

This new church that I was assigned to had been through a great deal of turmoil for nearly a decade. You name it; financial trouble, the facility, the facility was too large, depreciated equipment, church splits, and disagreements over direction and leadership. A real mess!

When we arrived, they had already reached full blown "survival mode" and their existence and purpose was simply to pay their bills each month. Month by month they would faithfully pay bills and watch the check book slowly dwindle and move closer and closer to the accounting red-zone.

What had once been a strong missions-giving church was now struggling to keep its lights on and the water connected. Survival mode is when your existence is to tread water as long as you can with high hopes of not drowning.

My wife and I felt strongly that this was the direction that God was leading our family. We were 99 percent sure we would be accepting this position, then, the board offered me what they could provide for me as the pay package and benefits. I remember clearly, I internally gasped for air, when I heard the amount of this pay package.

I remember that moment like it was yesterday. I looked at the paper and realized that I had not seen that small of a paycheck for over a decade. I would be making less than when I was a youth pastor a decade ago.

I gasped, I questioned, yet I accepted.

I was hoping that none of these church board members heard my flesh acting out, concerning my future welfare. I shuttered at the thought of trying to raise five kids on an entry level salary. I was having moments of disbelief and unquestionable fear as I signed on the dotted line to this new assignment.

Our first Sunday, 48 people worshipped together and celebrated Easter in a sanctuary that seated nearly 400 people. It was a surreal moment, the enemy was telling me lies like, "You're better than this. You could have a lot bigger church."

It did not take long for me to start believing the lies that the enemy was hurling at me and I was feeling like I may have not heard from God correctly and now I felt stuck in a hopeless situation.

Depression? Perhaps, not clinical depression. Just a good case of feeling sorry for myself and thinking too highly of myself and my gifts. "Why would God bring me here?"

What a silly question to ask God, is it not? "Why would God bring me here?"

The answer to this mystery that I was trying to unravel was found on every page of the Bible. From the very first page of the Bible, we see the message of the gospel unfolding, the Old Testament is a foreshadowing of things to come. Shadows in the Old Testament are pointing to the story of the New Covenant, which Jesus fulfills. In His teachings, He gave us the instruction known as the Great Commandment and he said that we should, "Love the Lord with all your heart, soul & mind." and "Love our neighbor as ourselves." In His teaching, known as the Great Commission, He says that we should, "Go into all the world and preach the gospel to every creature."

The answer to the question was simple... He called me here because He loves these people.

I fear the western church gets caught up in the idea that we are to climb the ladder of success with our calling. We will start out as a youth pastor, who then goes to some small rural community, gets some On-the-Job-Training (OJT) out in the boondocks, finds a better church in suburbia, then move to an even larger church that gives millions to missions and then you either retire, die, or work at Wal-Mart as the door-greeter.

Let this declaration remind you that you are called to obedience.

HE CALLED ME.

Even though it meant living in poverty.

Even if it meant trusting Him for my utilities bill.

HE CALLED ME to a small rural town because Jesus DIED for these people.

He loves them with an everlasting love, and he is drawing them back to him because of his loving kindness.

He does this through the 5-fold ministry found in Ephesians 4. These offices are known as the: "prophet" "apostle" "pastor" "teacher" and "evangelist." We need to be obedient to His call, and trust in the Lord with everything you have and believe that he will equip you for whatever task may come your way.

Let us take a closer look at the name pastor. The word "pastor" is not necessarily a title, as much as it is caregiver, shepherd, and friend to the sinners. I have never been able to see myself as a CEO of a corporation that manages a large staff. There are a lot of people who qualify to be a CEO or a business leader. I have been called by God with the highest calling known to man and this calling has an eternal purpose.

I believe my calling is to obedience and to sharing the gospel of God's grace. Therefore, I do not work for the church, the church board or even my denomination. I am a fully devoted follower of Christ, who is in an eternal covenant with God. I am accountable to the creator of the Universe and I have submitted myself to serving him even if it means I must deal with being uncomfortable. I have learned over the years that God is more concerned about me living under his covenant more than he is concerned about my desired comfort level.

Early on in my rural journey I realized that I did not have the tools I needed to correctly pursue this new passion in my life. I have enjoyed favor in ministry, balanced with a good dose of pain and fertile growing opportunities. The tools I needed were not so much in theological training, leadership development or preaching techniques. The tools I needed would require a different mind-set. Tools that allowed me to dream outside of the box, to teach me how to make friends in the community. I did not know how to relate to a small community that revolved around the school district as the hub of all local activity.

I was an outsider that did not know the local inside jokes or how important their yearly festivals were to the locals. God never gives us more than we can handle. Even though I felt like I was being swallowed up by some rural tornado of misunderstanding and feeling overwhelmed by all the tactical responsibilities to get this church back to some form of health and future dreaming.

God has come through for my family, our church and even the community more times than I can count.

His call is satisfying, and God is good.

Faithfully Serving Jesus,

John McHaffie
Small Church Pastor

Dear Small Church Pastor:

I love my family! I literally would do anything for my wife and five kids.

Every dad knows there are certain dates throughout the year that he had better not forget, birthdays, anniversaries, holidays, sporting events, and the last day of school.

My kids are like any other kids, they like to receive gifts on those special dates. Small or large gifts, it really does not matter, just a thoughtful "adda boy," birthday, holiday gift, or a surprise visit to a family-favorite restaurant causes my kids great pleasure.

We all need to admit, we all love gifts. Gifts are fun, gifts are good, and we love them.

God is a gift-giving Father that wants to give good gifts to his children. There are roughly 18,800 people groups in the world today. God longs to give good gifts to each of them.

We have been commissioned by the Word of God to spread the gospel of God's grace to each of these people groups. Some people have been called to cross the saltwater to fulfill their calling; some are called to the inner city, while some are called to teach on the university level in various locations around the globe. I personally have been called to rural churches and communities.

Rural ministry should never be a steppingstone, but a destination.

One of the most foundational scriptures in the Bible is John 3:16 "For God so loved the world, that he gave his only begotten Son, that whosoever believeth in him should not perish, but have everlasting life" (King James Bible 2021).

In this passage, we see that "God gave." God gave His son Jesus that the world would have an opportunity to come into a right relationship with Him and have eternal life in the presence of God himself. This behavior is born out of love, the unconditional affection that the creator of the universe has with his creation.

Giving is a characteristic of God.

He gives life. He gives breath. He gives hope. He gives us the desire to continue a life of obedience as we continue serving, caring, sharing, and loving the communities that surround us.

God gave His son so the world would have hope and not perish for an eternity. That is the conduct of a loving father. A loving father gives out of his love to each of his children.

Jesus in turn behaves in the same manner, John 5:19 "Jesus gave them this answer: 'Very truly I tell you, the Son can do nothing by himself; he can do only what he sees his Father doing, because whatever the Father does the Son also does'" (King James Bible 2021).

In the book of Ephesians 4:11-13 Paul writes these words, "So Christ himself gave the apostles, the prophets, the evangelists, the pastors and teachers, to equip his people for works of service, so that the body of Christ may be built up until we all reach unity in the faith and in the knowledge of the Son of God and become mature, attaining to the whole measure of the fullness of Christ" (King James Bible 2021).

Do you see this?

God gave His son!

Christ gave gifts to the church!

Take a closer look to what He gives! He gives a gift to the church, apostles, prophets, evangelist, pastors, and teachers.

Wow, what a gift!

This is a very common passage known as the 5-fold function of the church. Each of these functions is a gift from Jesus to the church. These tasks are not noted as being eternal, but temporal for us to use while we walk in obedience in the region God has positioned us to serve. He gives us the tools necessary for us to accomplish the Great Commission regionally. Do not be deceived, my beloved brethren.

James 1:16-17- "Every good thing given and every perfect gift is from above, coming down from the Father of lights, with whom there is no variation or shifting shadow" (King James Bible 2021). In the exercise of His will, He brought us forth by the word of truth, so that we would be a kind of first fruits among His creatures.

Our eternal function is "Sons of God." When we walk through the pearly gates, we will not be listed or known as apostles, prophets, evangelist, pastors, or teachers. We will be known as Sons of God. Those who are led by the Spirit of God are sons of God. For you did not receive a spirit that makes you a slave again to fear, but you received the Spirit who makes you sons. And by him we cry, "Abba, Father." Romans 8:14-15 NIV

But while we remain in this temporal body, we are given these functions to equip his people for works of service, so that the body of Christ may be built up.

Each of these gifts is extremely important to the church for equipping the body of Christ. However, I would like to focus on just one of these functions for a few minutes of your time.

The apostolic gift.

This is a function that is not overly recognized in our churches today for various reasons, one being abuse of this gift. When I mention the world apostolic you either had weird feelings, good feelings or some may have no feelings toward this gift.

I personally believe that the apostolic gift is an under used gift for lack of understanding of what it is supposed to be or how it behaves. The simplest definition is "sent one." I resonate with this definition and its perception of just that, being sent to a spiritually dark region.

During the 1800's, the United States of America was quickly moving from the northeast to a westerly direction to look for new land, to find gold in 'dem dar hills,' and to establish a nation with life, liberty, and the pursuit of happiness. Two types of people began to trek towards the west: Pioneers and Settlers.

Pioneers were the rough and tough characters that would ride horse back for day on end and were not afraid of the rattle snake, weather, or the Grizzly bear. As long as there was a horizon, they kept on riding and logging in their journals all their findings. They did not stop until they finally approached the exquisite beauty of the Pacific Ocean.

The other group was known as settlers. This group was as equally as tenacious, but with a different function. They did not have a desire driven by the horizon, but a desire to find local resources that would enhance the desire for the building of cities, marketplaces, and homes for this new generation of explorers to live and prosper.

The pioneer spirit is closely related to the apostolic spirit. Not settling for the finer things of life or for comforts and convenience, but willing to keep on moving towards the horizon of God's faithfulness in your call to obedience. What I am speaking about is not a physical pioneer or settler, but rather a spiritual pioneer that longs to see everything that God has in store for that region and geography.

The rural community should never be looked upon as a steppingstone to greater accomplishments for your personal portfolio and resume'. The rural church is a place, with real people, real needs and a place that needs a pioneer to keep searching and looking for what more God has in store. God is not finished with your region! He has more for you to do, more for you to accomplish, more for you to dream and Jesus has given this region to YOU. Your function as an apostolic leader is crucial for God to move mightily in your neck of the woods.

Let us take a closer look at the word apostle. The word apostle is from the Greek *"apostlos,"* which means "a delegate, messenger, one sent forth with orders." The apostles, formerly known as the disciples, were sent out by God and to preach the gospel to the world and they were told to make disciples of all nations.

Matthew 28:18-20 – "Then Jesus came to them and said, 'All authority in heaven and on earth has been given to me. Therefore go and make disciples of all nations, baptizing them in the name of the Father and of the Son and of the Holy Spirit, and teaching them to obey everything I have commanded you. And surely I am with you always, to the very end of the age.'

But you will receive power when the Holy Spirit comes on you; and you will be my witnesses in Jerusalem, and in all Judea and Samaria, and to the ends of the earth" Acts 1:8 (King James Bible 2021).

In a practical use of the word, modern day missionaries are identified as apostles, this term stems from the Latin equal of apostle, _missio_, where we get our English word for "missionary».

In most cases, we do not have a problem with the apostolic gift, as long as it is packaged in the Latin language. We love missionaries, we send missionaries, and we salute missionaries for going to the "ends of the earth" with the gospel of God's Grace.

Our local churches we generally support home missionaries as well as foreign missionaries as a general practice. Many of our home missionaries are serving the inner cities of America, teaching as professors in Native American colleges, compassion and disaster response and various children's and youth ministries, all of which are fantastic but not necessarily serving as a genuine apostolic role.

Most of which serve faithfully and effectively in the areas of pastor, evangelist, and teacher.

What I am hoping for in this writing is that you will "look and see" that the fields are white, ripe, and ready for harvest. I am praying to the Lord of the harvest to send apostles who labor in these rural harvest fields and believe for the greatest harvest ever recorded in church history.

Dr. George O. Wood in his April 2015 newsletter to pastors said, "There are thousands of "little strength" (AG News 2015) churches in the Assemblies of God. In fact, more than eight-thousand of our churches have less than one-hundred people."

Can you begin to imagine each of those pastors being empowered by the Holy Spirit and walking in Kingdom authority and claiming each of these regions to the glory of God instead of being a statistic of small church growth and numbers? We need an apostolic spark in the small, forgotten places and to begin to walk in the power and might of the Holy Spirit.

Jeff Hartensveld, in his book *Apostolic Spark* says, "Apostolic authority exists in the lives and relationships that are established when a church is planted in an unreached area."

Many of our rural American churches were established many years ago in unchurched areas, but because our churches are now established in these areas, we forget why they were planted. We must be reminded of the pioneer vision in those areas was to reach the lost, but most have settled for status quo and can't see the horizon anymore.

John Hartensveld defines the term apostle as, "God's groundbreaking pioneer to go to the regions beyond, His gift to humanity to finish the task of the Great Commission primarily as taking the good news of the Kingdom to every ethnicity" Matthew 28:19-20; Matthew 24:14; Acts 1:8.

He goes on to say, "While some may say my definition is too narrow, I believe this is the function for which God gave the gift of the apostle."

Hudson Taylor said, "I have found that there are three stages in every great work: first, it is impossible, then it is difficult, then it is done" (George 2014). I believe with you for your region that God would give you a fresh creative flow and innovation to accomplish your God-given-great-goal.

Faithfully Serving Jesus,

John McHaffie
Small Church Pastor

Dear Small Church Pastor,

few years ago, I received a phone call from the office of the Enrichment Journal and was asked to share my thoughts on the topic of compassion. I wanted to share these questions with you as well as my responses to these questions (Barra, de Jesus, McHaffie 2012).

What should the goal of your compassion ministries be?

Compassion ministry is more than just passing out a truckload of food. Compassion ministry is when we help the person at the gas station — we do things for people.

I worked with the City of Mount Vernon and Lawrence County a few years ago, an ice storm devastated our area. A Community Emergency Response Team was developed and that became part of the compassion ministry.

Also, many churches have a Wednesday night bus ministry where they pick up kids from rural areas and feed them a hot meal before church service.

Rural churches may not have significant resources. However, if you look hard enough you will find people who will help with your vision, shoes, coats, and school backpacks.

Do not be a lone ranger. Work with other pastors in the community to have a community service day on a weekend. It is wonderful to have a get-your-hands-dirty type of compassion ministry in your city.

How can I get members of my church interested in compassion ministry?

Some people may never emotionally experience compassion for the lost or compassion in general. Some people simply feel sorry for someone in need and do not do anything about it.

For me, it is a matter of discipleship. I train and teach compassion from the example of the Early Church. The Early Church started with compassion for widows and orphans.

Having this as part of our church's DNA is important. Compassion ministry is a lifelong pursuit.

What role does discipleship play in your compassion ministry in the local church?

Newer people coming into the church want to be part of compassion ministry. This is important in small town rural America — they want to be involved in something bigger.

Even those we have helped, or are still helping, want to be part of the process. Part of the discipleship process is getting people involved in some aspect of compassion ministries. We get them involved while still holding them accountable and supporting them.

Compassion ministry can be messy, as you incorporate the recipients into your church. How can I help regular attendees adjust to the new people coming into our church?

When I came to the rural church, the least, the last, and the lost were not the church's priority list. It was "we don't smoke, we don't chew, and we don't go with girls who do" type of church. I am learning that compassion ministry, in the rural setting, is tedious.

I keep reminding myself that people do not change overnight. If compassion ministry is to be a lifestyle of the church, I must keep selling the vision over and over again.

How can compassion ministry change the perception of your church in the community?

We change the community's perception of compassion at the grassroots level.

The rural Midwest is known as the Bible Belt. People think if you are not a Christian, you are at least born Catholic. So, compassion to me is Spirit-led kindness. It is not something we do. In some rural areas, churches have used compassion ministries to get people to come to their church and only their church.

Compassion ministry is not a means to simply get people through the front door of your church. We are compassionate because Jesus calls us to be compassionate. When I was at Central Bible College, I heard a chapel speaker say, "It's not about me. It's about Him, and it's about them." Since then, I have adopted this quote into one of my personal core values.

How do you fund your compassion ministries? What resources are available to pastors wanting to begin a ministry of compassion?

Thankfully, it takes more than money to fulfill the call to compassion. Faith and obedience are essential. A few people in the church who believe in the mission fund compose most of our compassion ministry. Other people will give money when we communicate a specific need by e-mail. For example, a lady in our church could not pay her electric bill. By the end of the day, we had more than enough to pay her electric bill. Compassion delivered that day.

Compassion might be as simple as going to the gas station and putting gas in someone's car or buying groceries for a single mother. One-on-one compassion ministry in rural areas is very effective. I teach people to do compassion daily, wherever they are to whomever.

Compassion workers can get discouraged or become cynical if they see people coming to the food pantry in an Escalade. How do you deal with that?

Romans 2:4 reminds us: "It is kindness that leads them to repentance" (King James Bible 2021). If they are in an Escalade, they still need Jesus. If they are scamming the system, maybe your kindness will be one step closer to them coming to Christ.

Faithfully Serving Jesus,

John McHaffie
Small Church Pastor

Dear Small Church Pastor,

*L*et us take a minute and address the need to dreaming big God-sized dreams.

No one ever said dreaming big dreams would be easy. If it were easy… go ahead and say it, everybody would be doing it!!

That is right. The sole purpose in having a big dream is because something inside of your spirit-man says you have a void in your ministry life and God wants to fix it. This new passion begins with fasting, prayer, bible study, and prayer times. A spiritual thought is birthed in your spirit-man and your normal reaction is usually to deny it or blame it on the pizza you had last evening before you went to bed.

A dream is something God births in the depths of your heart, a place that is safe but not necessarily the place that God intended for that dream to stay. D.L. moody is credited with this thought, "If God is your partner, make your plans big" (Moody 2012).

In the Bible, we see several times where a dream was given yet it took years for the dream to come to fruition. I think of heroes like Abraham, Joseph, Moses, Joshua, David, Esther, and a plethora of others too numerous to note in this paragraph.

A few letters ago I told you the story of a miracle that happened of how my church sold a church building.

Once all the paperwork was completed and signed it was time to move on to the next phase of the project, designing and building a new facility. I am sure some of you reading this and have been in a similar place. So, feel free to laugh at me and some of the circumstances we experienced as it brings your building memories to life again.

Who would have thought? Building codes, site plans, dirt tests, water-run off, and a host of other things would be my life for the next year or so.

Part of the process of learning is experimenting. Let me remind you that most experiments are just that, experiments for learning. Experiments lead us to places we never really wanted to go in the first place but have to if we want to get our new building finished.

You can imagine this scenario, five guys sitting around a small round table with our folders opened, coffee in one hand and a pencil in the other hand. We were eager to get this process started.

We discussed trying to use existing structures in our community for a few reasons. It was possibly less expensive to renovate, or to turn an existing community eye sore into something beautiful, but frankly this conversation was just a place for us to start this grueling process.

After a couple of months and a couple thousand dollars we moved away from the idea of purchasing existing structures and we purchased a small piece of land within the city limits. Our new three-acre plot was across from two of our schools, down the street from the hospital and on a major roadway, which led to high visibility to the locals.

The time had come...

We needed plans, building plans, not plans from a napkin or from someone's Google Sketch program. We needed architectural plans with an engineer stamp of approval.

Once we hired the architect, we realized we were not prepared for this process. This process took a better part of a year to get our necessary approvals and for us to begin the bidding process.

As the process went along, we witnessed the hand of God, as well as the enemy of our soul longing to kill, steal and destroy what God destined to build. There were several times along this process of building that our board meetings turned into prayer meetings, and we had to place the situation at Jesus' feet and just worship Him.

Yes, we did finish the building. Yes, we did build substantially smaller than before. Yes, we did end up with a state-of-the-art facility. Yes, we did end up with a manageable amount of debt. Yes, we were constantly growing. To God be the glory.

Dream God-sized dreams.

Faithfully Serving Jesus,

John McHaffie
Small Church Pastor

Dear Small Church Pastor,

I am closing out this series of letters by listing my 5 finest contributions to the world. I have experienced sleeping in a jungle, riding on planes trains and automobiles, I have led small groups, witnessed healings, preached many sermons, led worship, prayed with countless people, visited many hospital rooms, grieved at funerals, celebrated with beautiful new brides and grooms, fed many children, Chaplain in Emergency services, set on numerous committees, chaired many board meetings, played on the worship team, built buildings, remodeled old church buildings and been active in each community that I have served. But the five greatest things I have given to the world is my Children.

Joshua is my oldest and firstborn son. I have observed God's hand on him as he has developed into an extremely intelligent and passionate worshipper. His passion for worship equals with passion for one-on-one discipleship. I want to speak Joshua 1:7-8 over his life and ministry; "Be strong and very courageous. Be careful to obey all the law my servant Moses gave you; do not turn from it to the right or to the left, that you may be successful wherever you go. Keep this Book of the Law always on your lips; meditate on it day and night, so that you may be careful to do everything written in it. Then you will be prosperous and successful."

Timothy is our second son and what a true blessing he is to our family. He is smart, strong, and witty, which has been developed as survival tactics in our large family. When he walks into the room, he lights it up with his energy and humor. Timothy has the ability to become anything his sets his heart on to do. I am speaking 1 Timothy 4:12-14 into his life, "Don't let anyone look down on you because you are young, but set an example for the believers in speech, in conduct, in love, in faith and in purity. Until I come, devote yourself to the public reading of Scripture, to preaching and to teaching. Do not neglect your gift, which was given you through prophecy when the body of elders laid their hands on you."

Emily is our only girl, and she has enjoyed the title as my favorite daughter. Emily has had her share of difficulties, from overcoming cancer to basic girl drama, I have watched her develop into a strong leader. Watch out world, here she comes! She is not afraid to tackle difficult situations and not afraid to stand her ground, the verse I pray over her is found in Psalm 27:1, "The LORD is my light and my salvation; whom shall I fear? The LORD is the stronghold of my life; of whom shall I be afraid" (King James Bible 2021)?

Tyler is gifted in patience and joy. He is the fourth of five kids. He too is smart, handsome, and witty, but he displays a calmness that I have not seen in his other siblings. He loves a good joke, or a fun binge series. However, he is drawn to the Word of God, but not out of obligation, but out of innocence and hunger. I am praying John 15:5, "I am the vine; you are the branches. If you remain in me and I in you, you will bear much fruit; apart from me you can do nothing" (King James Bible 2021).

Caleb is an amazing human being. He has had four older siblings to show him the ropes for good and for bad. He loves singing worship music, talking about God, science, and he questions everything. I love the long, deep conversations we have while he assists me in life and ministry. Caleb has the ability to turn the world upside down and he will have the family support to do whatever God has called him to do. I am praying Philippians 1:6 "...being confident of this, that he who began a good work in you will carry it on to completion until the day of Christ Jesus" (King James Bible 2021).

Let us keep on keeping on for His glory, you are a blessing to your community, church and beyond! Now I will conclude by praying this passage over you, "Hear, O Israel: The Lord our God, the Lord is one. Love the Lord your God with all your heart and with all your soul and with all your strength. These commandments that I give you today are to be on your hearts. Impress them on your children. Talk about them when you sit at home and when you walk along the road, when you lie down and when you get up. Tie them as symbols on your hands and bind them on your foreheads. Write them on the doorframes of your houses and on your gates." Deuteronomy 6:4-9 (King James Bible 2021).

Faithfully serving Jesus,

John McHaffie
Small Church Pastor

Works Cited

2021. *Pick a File.* February 4. https://download-pdfs.com/v6/preview/?pid=6&offer_id=430&ref_id=61fc281ca-8f0e9ed72cc5623GC5e3Zoz_63465ea5_ec371366&-sub1=63465ea5&keyword=A%20Priest%20to%20the%20Temple,%20Or,%20the%20Country%20Parson%20His%20Character,%20and%20Rule%20of%20.

Australia, Hillsong Music. 2001. *God is Great.* Cond. You are My World. Comp. Hillsong Worship.

Barclay, William. 2016. "The Pursuit of Excellence." By Mary Meadows, 3. LULU Publishing.

Barnett, Tommy. 2012. *Strategic Church: A Life-Changing Church in an Ever Changing .* United States: Baker Publishing Group.

Batterson, Mark. 2016. *The Circle Maker.* ISBN: Zondervan.

Briggs, Katharine C. 1987. "Myers-Briggs Type Indicator." *Consulting Psychologists Press.*

Capricorn, Jesus was a. 1972. *Why Me.* Cond. Monument Records. Comp. Kris Kristofferson.

2021. "Catholic Encyclopedia ." *Catholic Answers.* February 4. https://www.catholic.com/encyclopedia.

2021. *Convoy of Hope.* February 4. https://www.convoyofhope.org/what-we-do/rural-compassion/.

2004. *Foxe's Book of Martyrs.* Emerald House Group, Incorporated.

Francis A. Schaeffer, Udo W. Middelman. 2003. *No Little People.* United States: Crossway.

George, David. 2014. "The Daily Thought Shaker." United States: Author Solutions .

Israel, Steve. 2013. *Charge! History's Greatest Military Speeches.* United States: Naval Institute Press.

2021. "Jeff Foxworthy Quotes." *Brainy Quote.* February 4. https://www.brainyquote.com/authors/jeff-foxworthy-quotes.

2014. *Jesus Freaks.* Baker Publishing Group.

2021. "King James Bible." *King James Bible Online.* February 4. https://www.kingjamesbibleonline.org/.

Pacitti, Michael. 2015. "A Great Lesson From Geese in V-Formation [video[." *https://www.youtube.com/watch?v=BBxHQp-WI97I&t=3s.* YouTube, September 13.

2011. "Pure and Simple Gaither." United States: Alfred Publishing Group.

Rocky Barra, Wilfredo De Jesus, and John McHaffie. 2012. "THE ASSEMBLIES OF GOD - THE PRACTICE OF MISSION - INTERVIEW WITH WILFREDO DE JESUS, ROCKY BARRA, AND JOHN MCHAFFIE." *ENRICHMENT JOURNAL.*

Ross, Tiffany. United States. *A Servant's Heart: 180 Encouraging Thoughts for Church Volunteers.* 2012: Barbour Publishing .

Smith, Michael W. 1990. *The Circle Maker.* Cond. Reunion. Comp. Michael W. Smith.

Sparrow/Sixstep. 2004. *How Great is our God.* Cond. Arriving. Comp. Chris Tomlin.

United States. *The Voice Bible: Step Into the Story of Scripture.* 2012: Thomas Nelson.

1996. *There is a Miracle in Your House.* Charisma House.

Wiersbe, Warren W. 2007. *On Being a Servant of God.* United States: Baker Publishing Group.

Wood, Dr. George O. 2015. "AG News." *Newsletter.* Assemblies of God World Missions, April.

CPSIA information can be obtained
at www.ICGtesting.com
Printed in the USA
BVHW081127010721
610975BV00007B/281